RECOLLECTIONS

Nathaniel Hailes' adventurous life in

colonial South Australia

Allan Peters is fascinated by history, and has a passion for
researching personalities. His first book, *No Monument
of Stone*, told the story of Elizabeth Woolcock, the only
woman ever executed in an Adelaide gaol. Allan lives
in Christies Beach where he and his artist wife, Pauline,
raised their two daughters.

WAKEFIELD PRESS

RECOLLECTIONS

Nathaniel Hailes' adventurous life in
colonial South Australia

Edited by
ALLAN L. PETERS

Wakefield Press
16 Rose Street
Mile End
South Australia 5031
www.wakefieldpress.com.au

First published 1998
Reprinted in 2020

Introduction and original research copyright © Allan L. Peters, 1998

All rights reserved. This book is copyright. Apart from any fair dealing for the purposes of private study, research, criticism or review, as permitted under the Copyright Act, no part may be reproduced without written permission. Enquiries should be addressed to the publisher.

Publisher's editor Gina Inverarity
Designed by Nick Stewart, design BITE, Adelaide
Typeset by Clinton Ellicott, MoBros, Adelaide

National Library of Australia
Cataloguing-in-publication entry

Recollections: Nathaniel Hailes' adventurous life in colonial South Australia 1802-1879.

Includes index.
ISBN 978 1 86254 467 3.

1. Hailes, Nathaniel, 1802-1879. 2. Pioneers - South Australia - Biography. I. Peters, Allan L., 1934-   .

994.2302092

CONTENTS

	INTRODUCTION	VII

episode

I	SELF TRANSPORTATION	1
II	ADELAIDE IN 1839	8
III	OUR EARLY BUILDINGS	15
IV	A TRANSPLANTED VILLAGE	23
V	MY FIRST ACQUAINTANCE WITH NATIVES	28
VI	FIRST GLIMPSES OF THE BUSH	34
VII	TWO WRECKS; THE *FANNY* AND *MARIA*	41
VIII	MURDER OF JOHN GOFTON	48
IX	THE UNEXPLORED BUSH	57
X	WATER AND THE WANT OF IT	64
XI	POSTAL COMMUNICATION	71
XII	OLD COLONIAL WEATHER	79

CONTENTS

XIII	COLONIAL PROGRESSION	95
XIV	THE GENERAL SCATTERING	103
XV	MURDERS AT PORT LINCOLN	109
XVI	RECONCILIATION OF TRIBES	117
XVII	PREHISTORIC COLONIAL SCENES	123
XVIII	BILL BRIEN, A HUMAN ENIGMA	129
XIX	SETTLING DOWN IN A NEW TOWN	135
XX	NATIVES IN THEIR PRIMITIVE CONDITION	143
XXI	ADDITIONAL CHARACTERISTICS OF NATIVES	150
XXII	THE FATAL JOURNEY OF C.C. DUTTON	159
XXIII	UNSUCCESSFUL SEARCH FOR DUTTON	168
	NOTES	177
	AUTHOR'S NOTE	178
	INDEX	179

INTRODUCTION

In 1876 Nathaniel Hailes, who was then aged seventy-four, set out to write what he referred to as his 'personal recollections'. He was no stranger to the literary world, for as a young man he had worked in his father's publishing house in London. He was also a recognised poet, and under the name of Timothy Short, and possibly other pseudonyms, wrote satire for a variety of short-lived South Australian newspapers. As late as 1873, whilst living in Mt Gambier, the seventy-one year-old still listed his occupation as 'reporter'.

The first twenty-four episodes of his recollections were about his life in England and were published in the *South Australian Register* commencing 15 December 1876 and concluding 7 July 1877.

The South Australian public read these colourful and descriptive pieces with great enthusiasm. As a consequence, Nathaniel was encouraged to continue the series by writing his recollections of life and events in the early days of South Australia's colonisation. They were quickly recognised as being among the most accurate sources of information about historical events of significance to this State.

In editing Nathaniel's recollections I have endeavoured to retain his original, unique style and humour, changing only words that are no longer in common usage, and in so doing trying to ensure that it once more becomes the free-flowing, easy-to-read work that it formerly was. Poems and most names have been reproduced verbatim.

On Nathaniel Hailes' death, in 1879, the *South Australian Register* published the following obituary:

DEATH OF MR NATHANIEL HAILES

At the ripe age of seventy-six years, and after a career in the colony marked by more than ordinary vicissitudes, Mr Nathaniel Hailes has passed away. His life almost naturally divides itself into two parts – the one half having been spent in England, the other half in South Australia. What his history was, both in the old country and in this new land where he ended his days, we in measure know from the deeply interesting records which were published in the *Register* in 1877–1878 under the title of 'Personal Recollections of a Septuagenarian', and which we now may say were from the pen of the deceased gentleman. According to these recollections he was, while in England, 'brought into contact with a great many eminent and interesting individuals and witnessed many extraordinary events which have now become history'.

Born in London in the year 1802, and dwelling there for about thirty-six years, he was so situated as to be acquainted with the circumstances connected with some of the most remarkable events, and to be on terms more or less intimate with many of the greatest minds of the past generation. He lived far enough back into the century to witness the adaptation of gas to street-lighting; to remember the exciting battle of Waterloo, and to have seen its two great heroes – Wellington and Blucher. He was on sufficiently friendly relations with Lady Byron as to dissuade her from publishing a treatise she wanted to publish on female education, and he had the privilege of seeing Mrs Siddons when she was in the zenith of her popularity as an actress. He was placed in a position which gave him frequent opportunities of meeting men like William Hazlitt, the Rev. Rolland Hill, Allan Cunningham, Edward Irving, Dr Chalmers, Sir Walter Scott, and other celebrities of a bygone age; and perhaps no one in the colony knew more of the inner life of the great minds which ruled the literary and theological world during the first forty years of the present century.

INTRODUCTION

Towards the close of 1838 Mr Hailes was appointed Superintendent of emigrants by the *Buckinghamshire*, which left Portsmouth on 10 December of that year, and reached Holdfast Bay in March 1839. In his 'Recollections' he tells how he 'beheld the conversion of a wilderness into the abode of an enlightened and prosperous community'; and the story he has left behind has supplied us with a chapter in the history of the colony which would otherwise most probably have been lost. For some time he carried on the business of an auctioneer, and his advertisements are remembered even now by old colonists as rivalling in their eloquence the noted literary efforts of George Robbins of London. He was also a regular contributor to the Press under the *nom de plume* of 'Timothy Short', and at one period started a newspaper – the *Adelaide Free Press* – which only existed a short time. On retiring from business at the end of 1842, he was appointed by Governor Grey to the office of Secretary to the Government Resident at Port Lincoln. Here his official duties brought him into close contact with the aborigines, and the *Register* of those days contains many interesting productions of his pen on aboriginal customs, life, and manners. When the establishment at Boston Bay was broken up, Mr Hailes lost his position, but afterwards filled the post of Secretary to the South Australian Institute Library, which he held for some years, and then received an appointment to the Labour Prison at Dry Creek. Upon relinquishing that position he moved to Mount Gambier, but after a limited residence there he returned to Adelaide, where he spent the remainder of his days. In 1841-42 he was a member of the City Council, and in 1842 he was a member of the Provisional Committee of the Society which was formed to secure religious freedom. These, as far as we know, are about the only public positions he held, but as a writer both of prose and poetry, he exercised in years gone by, considerable influence.

episode

I

South Australian Register 8 January 1878

SELF TRANSPORTATION

In the year 1838 I had reached a major cross-road in my life, and the world was all before me. Where should I choose to be? I found myself at liberty to ask. In the old world of England? In the new world of America? Or in the newer new world of Australia? I turned my thoughts to New Zealand, and after having had an interview with Colonel Campbell, who had been charged with governing that colony, and was about to depart England to fulfil that role, I decided instead on Australia.

Why I chose this then infantine settlement was attributable to several causes. I had just read Captain Sturt's interesting work; had been preceded to the colony by several old friends, among whom were the late Mr William Giles, Manager of the South Australian Company, and Mr A.H. Davis of the Reedbeds; and moreover, I had recently been introduced to Mr Robert Gouger, who had spent some months in the colony and returned temporarily to England, and who, of course, was able to answer enquiries about it from personal knowledge. He supplied me with several 'wrinkles', as they are called, one or two of which without any fault on his part misled me. Among other things, he advised me to procure a plentiful supply of double sole and double upper leather boots, and referred me to the artisan by whom he had been supplied with similar articles.

With a dozen pairs of these I armed or rather legged myself, setting speargrass at defiance.

When I arrived in South Australia at the end of the unusually dry summer of 1838 I looked on the hard smooth, dark-brown surface of the land and was only prevented from laughing by recollections of the cost of my boots, which I subsequently disposed of at half the sum. Had I arrived six months earlier, when tough, strong speargrass was from two to three feet high, I should no doubt have felt grateful to Mr Gouger for his sound advice. In assessing such statements the time and circumstances under which they are made must be taken into account. The River Torrens for instance was described by some early visitors as a foaming torrent and by others as an insignificant stream – season no doubt accounting for the difference. Horton James published a book in London in 1839 titled *Six months in South Australia*, which contained some unpalatable truths intermingled with many great absurdities. It stated amongst other things that 'the river would flow through an Irishman's hat'. I personally have not seen an Irishman's hat, nor indeed a hat belonging to a man of any nationality, of such great proportion.

The colonists of South Australia are deeply indebted to the small but resolute and intelligent band of pioneers through whose exertions it became a British colony. Among these Robert Gouger especially distinguished himself. He with others succeeded in obtaining the favourable attention of Lord Stanley, who was then in power, and also of the most unlikely man in England, the Duke of Wellington. The Duke, usually looking at the matter of colonisation solely from a military point of view, was opposed to extensive emigration, as depleting England of material for the British army and navy in the event of war. Yet he favoured this particular undertaking and by his personal influence obtained the Royal assent to the Bill on the very last day of the session, but for which indefinite delay must have occurred. The following copy of a letter from the Duke, written subsequent to the passing of the Act, proves that he felt kindly towards the infant colony.

> London, 2 September 1835
>
> Sir — I have had the honour of receiving your letter of this day. I am much concerned that it will be quite impossible for me to comply with the desire of the gentlemen who have commissioned you to invite me to dine with them on Thursday, the 10th of this month. If Parliament should still be sitting I shall certainly be engaged in its business, if not, I am engaged to go out of town immediately to give my attendance upon other public affairs, which it is my duty not to neglect. Under these circumstances I trust that the gentlemen interested in the colonisation of South Australia will excuse me for declining to promise to attend their meeting. I beg at the same time, in answer to that part of your letter in which you have adverted to the course which I took in the House of Lords on the Bill relating to their objects, to say that I feel a great anxiety that the plan which has been adopted may succeed, and may contribute to the happiness and prosperity of the colonists and to the advantage of all concerned
>
> I have &c.,
Wellington
>
> R. Gouger, Esq.
> 5, Hind-Street, Manchester Square

In November, 1838, I secured cabins in the *Buckinghamshire*, one of the fine old East Indiamen, of I think near 1700 tons and preparatory to going on board intended to make a circuit through the midland counties of England for the purpose of taking leave of relatives. Perhaps it was as well for me that an incident occurred which rendered this impracticable; for taking leave, when the separation is almost sure to be final, is painfully dry work, or if moistened with tears, is more painful still. A day or two after a friend of mine received a letter from Colonel Torrens stating that the gentleman who had been appointed Superintendent of Emigrants on board the *Buckinghamshire* had been compelled by domestic circumstances to decline the voyage and enquiring if my friend thought that I would accept the charge. A letter from the Adelphi reached me next day offering me the billet, and requesting that whatever my decision might be I would call on the Commissioners on the following day at an hour named. I at once determined to decline the offer, the little time at my disposal prior to the sailing of the *Buckinghamshire* being scarcely sufficient for completion of my private arrangements, but I attended as requested at the Adelphi on the following forenoon. I was engaged in conversation with Mr Rowland Hill some half-hour before being introduced to the Commissioners. He explained to me the dilemma in which the Commissioners were placed, and in an effort to procure my acceptance of the billet, used his persuasive powers to the utmost, but in vain. In the Commissioners' room I was at length persuaded to say 'Yes,' and before I left, Mr Hill handed me comprehensive instructions which had been prepared for another, whose name was struck out to make room for mine. Emigrants had already begun to assemble at Deptford, and the less important of my own affairs had to yield to those of the depot.

Good-bying was nipped in the bud. Thanks to the railway which was then in progress between London and Birmingham, I was enabled to pay a brief visit to relatives there, but not to extend visits therefrom. That was the first long line of rail which I traversed. The lines were commenced from either end, and would on completion of the work meet midway between the two cities, so we steamed from London to Rugby, where we were bundled into stage-coaches, spring-carts, postchaises, and half a dozen other sorts of vehicles, which conveyed us sixteen miles, when we reached the line approaching from Birmingham. There is a tunnel some mile in length between London and Rugby, and entrance to that in those inexperienced days certainly created a novel sensation. The darkness of the elongated arch, relieved at intervals by shafts of light from above, had if not an unearthly certainly an un-English aspect. To mend the matter, the up train met us in the middle of the tunnel, and the mingled rumble had a weird earthquaking sort of effect. An old lady sat next to me, and on our entrance to the tunnel she laid her head on my shoulder, threw her arms around me as tightly as the most ardent affection could have dictated, and remained perfectly silent until we emerged into daylight. She then asked, 'What did you think?' I replied, 'I thought that you and I and the rest of us resembled shots being propelled from a duck gun.' But she had evidently been in great terror, and did not approve of jesting on so serious a subject.

On the 6th December 1838, I went on board the *Buckinghamshire*, which was anchored a little below Gravesend. The number of emigrants then on board of both sexes and of all ages was three hundred and three. On the 10th, off Portsmouth, the remainder were received on board, making the full complement four hundred and forty-seven. After an exceptionally fine passage we anchored in Holdfast Bay on 22nd March, 1839. Most travellers are very dramatic when describing their sea voyages. They dish up for the reader's enjoyment storms, calms, seagulls, flying fish, albatrosses, sharks, water-spouts and other spouts including speeches and sea-sickness; but I have more consideration for my readers, and hasten to arrive at the 'Great South Land'. We saw no land between Madeira and Kangaroo Island except the small island of St Paul's. From the large number of persons on board I had abundant occasion for psychological observation. The fanciful anticipations of some of the eager colonists were very edifying. It was my duty, on nearing land, to encourage them to the utmost, and I quite elevated the hearts of a large group, consisting chiefly of females, by convincing them that among the trees on Kangaroo Island they discerned the spire of a church; and if I had been in possession of John Philpot Curran's telescope I have no doubt I could have enabled them to hear bass-viols, flutes, clarionets, and vocal psalmody – an organ probably would have been too large an article for them to swallow.

One passenger, a Sussex farmer, amused me greatly. He was a Dandie Dinmont in his way; a fine, powerful, frank, warm-hearted and simple-minded fellow. He subsequently acquired good property in the colony, but died comparatively young. His particular idiosyncrasy was dread of the natives. Immediately after we had cast anchor in Holdfast Bay Mr Elles came to me clad in his Sunday clothes for wear ashore, to wit, a blue coat with brass buttons, yellow waistcoat with similar brass buttons, and breeches, and top boots, and enquired of me 'Mr Hailes, what be they black things on the shore yonder?' I answered, 'They are native Aborigines,' and looking through the ship's telescope, added, 'and fine athletic fellows they are.' 'Well now,' said Elles, 'if I meet any of them Bodginees when I get ashore I'll shoot 'em that I will.' (He had his loaded rifle on his arm.) 'Now do you think the Governor would do anything to me for shooting Bodginees?' 'Oh!' I replied, 'he would hang you, that's all.' 'Would he now! What a shame!' was his response. Years after I saw many natives at work on his freehold and laughed with him about his former terrors.

On reaching the Glenelg beach, which as we all know, shallows so gradually that sea boats cannot go close in, a brawny piece of human ebony some six feet high, named Rodney, approached the astounded farmer, offering to bear him on his shoulders to the shore, as he had already borne several others. The newly arrived colonist was indignant, and demanded that one of the boat's crew should perform the duty. This demand was acceded to, and a burly sailor, apparently equal to carry a church, took Elles on his shoulders, when strange to say, both disappeared under water, and the blue coat, yellow waistcoat cord breeches, top boots and loaded rifle, together with the owner of that miscellaneous collection of chattels, were rolled in the surf, whence however, they were rescued in due time. Of course the occurrence was purely accidental!

My experiences on shore must be reserved for another episode.

episode

II

South Australian Register 15 January 1878

ADELAIDE
IN 1839

What a fantastic sensation it is to set one's feet on solid land after a lengthy sea voyage. Even the apparent efforts of the beach to imitate the undulations of the ocean could not dampen this feeling of elation. And when the spot on which you have set your feet gives entrance to a desert on the opposite side of the globe from that which you left a few months before, the sensation acquires a romantic element. You feel that you have done something heroic in leaving a civilised land to come to where swans are black instead of white. Where indigenous quadrupeds travel in leaps, erect on their hind legs, instead of walking or running on all four. Where trees shed their bark instead of their leaves, and rivers flow sometimes underground, sometimes on the surface, and instead of broadening as they near the ocean, narrow to a trickle or disappear completely as they approach it. Where the aboriginal population, instead of sporting the orthodox white and red, have skins the colour of the finest quality ebony.

Though the road from Glenelg to the site of Adelaide was little more than a torturous, winding track created by the footsteps of numerous earlier pedestrians and the few haulage animals and vehicles that serviced the town, I enjoyed the experience of my first walk in the new colony. The narrow track meandered along amid an apparently boundless maze of strongly scented shrubs and magnificent gum-trees. The branches of the trees were crowded and enlivened by flocks of parrots, cockatoos and parroquets, whose coloured and varied plumage rendered the scene immensely picturesque. As yet the multitude of white, blue and yellow flowers, which I was to behold on this very same spot a few months later, were cradled and temporarily hidden beneath the bare and apparently sterile surface of the earth. Flocks of screaming, chattering birds frolicked like feathered monkeys and accompanied every traveller or group of gaping wayfarers for miles, keeping always a little in advance and scrutinising each individual with a rigorous eye. Here and there a laughing-jackass gave forth its mocking laugh, as if to scoff, and ridicule each new trespasser to its territory.

Now and then the gentler, sweetly simple strains of smaller birds were to be heard. Those who say that this country is lacking in song-birds can never have wandered in its more secluded woodlands. True, we have no songbirds whose sustained and elaborate harmonies rival those of Europe's most boasted melodists, but we have many whose simpler strains delight the ear and touch the heart of those who would but listen. They who are accustomed to the remote bush will be aware that several of our meek little vocalists continue their summer song far into the night if the moon be shining, or if intervening vapour does not tarnish the brightness of the stars.

But my present theme is Adelaide, the future city. The condition of the settlement had not much varied when I arrived, in the early part of the year 1839, to that described by Mr Horton James in his written account of it as beheld by him in 1838. The first sign of civilisation to be seen was a number of rudimentary huts along the town's northern boundary. They were made of reeds from the nearby Torrens River and as I later discovered were collectively referred to as Buffalo Row, after the vessel in which their first residents arrived.

Soon after passing these huts more buildings came into view, firstly small huts and cottages, then sprinkled here and there a few more substantial buildings. One quite enormous structure belonging to the South Australian Company, another good brick house to Mr Hack, another to the enterprising Mr Gilles, one to Mr Thomas, and a couple of new taverns. But in the main the rest of the dwellings were small and made of very light materials; and the number of canvas tents and marquees gave some parts of the settlement the appearance of a camp.

Most of the newcomers settle down on what is called the Park Lands, where they are handy to the rivulet, and they construct a Robinson Crusoe sort of hut with twigs and branches from the adjoining forest. In this fine and dry climate these huts answer well enough as temporary residences. The principal streets have been laid out in the survey of the town and are 132 feet wide, which is nearly twice as wide as Portland-place, and the squares are all so large, that if there were any inhabitants in them a cab would almost be required to get across them.

Some critics of the Surveyor's design for the town, especially in regard to the enormously wide streets, the expansive squares and surrounding belt of parklands, openly complained of wasted space. 'And how will the case stand 50 years hence,' they asked, 'seeing that by Act of Parliament the limit of the city can never be extended?' Certainly at the outset the large extent of bush-like township often occasioned much individual inconvenience. People began to build in all parts of it and very small villages and solitary houses were scattered here and there. I remember during the first conversation I had with Captain Sturt, offering a suggestion that strict regulations should be enforced to ensure that the town should progress in a more orderly fashion extending gradually from the centre to the four terraces. Captain Sturt concurred with the suggestion, as he did with another that I made with due course. My idea was that if the city had been placed wholly on the northern side of the river on a portion of the raised tableland which extends from Montefiore Hill to Dry Creek, the plain on which South Adelaide stands would have been a more suitable suburb for dairy farms and the production of fruit, flowers and culinary vegetables. However, when told of this among complaints from a variety of sources, Colonel Light was adamant that his original plan was to be adhered to in every respect. Time alone will determine the wisdom or otherwise of his unflinching determination.

But my present business is with Adelaide as I found it in the month of March, 1839. At that time it resembled an extensive gipsy encampment. Not the semblance of a street existed on the land, although all the main streets had been duly laid down on the plan. It was in fact an extensive woodland, with here a solitary tent and there clusters of erratic habitations. There were canvas tents, calico tents, tarpaulin tents, wurleys made of branches, log huts, packing case villas, and a few veritable wooden cottages, amid which here and there appeared some good houses. One of these had been erected for Mr Charles Mann, the first Advocate-General. I think the acre fronted Brown Street [Morphett Street]; the house faced a picturesque portion of the Mount Lofty range of hills, the view of which was not interrupted by intervening timber and was thus placed for the sake of the prospect. 'Will the house face the street when the street is made apparent?' I asked of Mr Mann the first afternoon I spent with him, towards the end of March, 1839. 'I think not,' he said, 'but it will face those hills.' Some months later when trees growing in the lines of streets were grubbed up, and fences defined boundaries, the house looked askew from the thoroughfare. That evening we sat beneath a gum tree in front of the house until a flock of raucous parrots had gone to roost in the branches above us and the last rays of the setting sun were fading on the opposite range of hills. That evening I was made acquainted, in Mr Mann's rapid and energetic style, with 'the short and simple annals' of the colony. Every event which had agitated the Lilliputian community from the date of proclamation was narrated to me. A photographic sketch of every prominent actor in scenes which then constituted the colonial drama taken of course from the sketcher's individual point of view, was supplied to me. That I did not retain all the information thus received was my own fault. Certainly that was the most pleasant evening I had yet spent in the forest of Adelaide.

It was easy to lose oneself in the heavily wooded city even in the daytime and at night it was scarcely possible to avoid doing so. The maze-like character of the spot was greatly enhanced by a multitude of wattles, which occupied spaces between gum or she-oak trees. Many instances occurred of people having to 'bush it', as the term was, all night within the limits of the town, or of going bewildered to their own residences to enquire the way home. After the grubbing up of trees commenced, town travelling after dark became even more precarious. There were pitfalls and man-traps in all directions and very few colonists of that date remained unacquainted with all of them. I will relate one instance as a sample of many similar misadventures. One very rainy evening I was proceeding to my home in Gilbert Street from the residence of Dr Nash in Grenfell Street, duly furnished with a lantern as well as an umbrella, when I unexpectedly walked into a cold bath, the surface of which just failed to reach my chin. From the uncomfortable sensation I experienced I sincerely hoped that I was the first bather therein – a hope no doubt well founded, for no previous rain had fallen since the removal of my predecessor in the hole, an enormous gum tree. I forget now what became of my lantern and umbrella, but I scrambled out somehow.

For years there was a laugh against Mr Jickling, who on my arrival was acting as Judge in place of Sir John Jeffcott, who at the end of 1837 was drowned at the entrance to the River Murray. I will retell the tragedy before the farce.

This fatal accident is the more to be regretted because it appears to have been partly caused by negligence or worse. The following is an extract from an official report to the Governor by Messrs. Strangways and Hutchinson:

> *12 December, 1937 – Captain Blenkinsop having returned to us from the fishery started in the whaleboat accompanied by Sir John Jeffcott to recross the bar. Having arrived at the narrowest part of the channel they proceeded two miles up the eastern channel, where on Hindmarsh Island, they found a makeshift flagpole erected. This they took down and having put a flag on it, erected it again. Soon after they found some hundredweights of whalebone, which they packed forward in the boat. The water at the entrance runs obliquely from the western to the opposite point, escaping to the S E. They had nearly passed all the breakers, when the boat filled and Sir John Jeffcott, Captain Blenkinsop and two of the boat's crew were drowned. It appeared afterwards that the boat's crew had concealed from Captain Blenkinsop the danger and difficulty they met with on entering, a knowledge of which might have prevented this melancholy catastrophe. Natives assisted the survivors by wading into the water, and dragging them nearly exhausted, to shore. On arriving among the breakers the necessity of providing for their safety caused the sounding to be neglected so that nothing is known of the depth of water there.*

This sad accident left South Australia without a duly appointed Judge until March 1939, when Judge Cooper arrived. The Acting Judge was an amiable and learned man, but suffered both from defective vision and hearing. He had been dining one day with Mr Osmond Gilles at his house, near St Johns Church, his own residence being in Gilles Arcade, about a mile distant. Another two guests who left Mr Gilles long after were surprised at overtaking Mr Jickling a very short distance from the starting point. He was standing before the trunk of a she-oak, the top of which had been lopped to a height of about five foot six inches. Bowing very politely and addressing the tree, he said 'Will you have the kindness to tell me the way to Gilles Arcade?' Of course the tree made no reply. Again bowing, he said, 'Do oblige by telling me the way to Gilles Arcade.' The tree was as mute as before. He pleaded a third time even more earnestly but with the same result, he then turned away on his uncertain journey, meekly remarking, 'Well, if you don't know the way you might at least have had the politeness to tell me so.' A loud laugh from the unsuspected spectators assured him of immediate and safe guidance to his not too distant residence, and many a good roasting at subsequent gatherings.

Of course, amid so many impromptu residences many curious scenes occurred. I remember one moonlight night as I was walking home a whirlwind swept across the scene, treating the lighter structures very unceremoniously. Some huts were utterly capsized and destroyed; while several tents were blown right away, pursued by their unfortunate owners, dressed in an amusing array of night attire not usually designed to be worn in public.

episode

III

South Australian Register 23 January 1878

OUR EARLY BUILDINGS

People now arriving in the colony [1878] find it difficult to procure residences, but in the early part of 1839 it was in most instances simply impossible to do so. Families walked from the seaside to the wooded plains, and settled down on the most pleasant spots they could find unoccupied. The sites nearest the Torrens River were by far the most popular, for the river supplied the indispensable water. If the weather were fine the first few nights on arrival would be spent under the lee side of a gum-tree with no canopy save the clear radiant sky. It was not at all uncommon for a kangaroo to blunder into the campsites within the town. Even as recently as 1840 a regular 'boomer' was killed at the back of a cottage in which I lived at North Adelaide, and a short time prior to that, one had been captured near King William Street.

I was particularly fortunate as far as shelter was concerned. Friends who had preceded me to the colony secured a cottage for me, which had previously been the Bank of South Australia. It was situated on North Terrace, covering a portion of the spot now occupied by the residence of Dr Gosse. [On the southern side, between King William Street and Stephens Place]. It consisted of three weatherboard rooms, with a hole about three feet square and five feet deep sunk in one of them, where the strong box used to be kept. This small cellar was useful for stowing away articles that needed to be kept cool. There was neither outhouse of any kind nor fireplace, and the rent was only £60 per annum. Great regard had been paid to ventilation as far as the roof was concerned. The shingles, having dried out somewhat since installation, no longer fitted tightly together and thus permitted the exhausted internal air to escape through the ensuing spaces between them. It was glorious on summer nights to be on one's back and watch the stars shining brightly overhead. When the heavy rains began to descend the arrangement was not altogether so pleasant, and I found a gig-umbrella that I had brought with me from England of special service. It was scarcely the thing, though, to pay £60 per annum for sleeping under one's own umbrella; so I speedily exchanged the first bank built in Adelaide for another notable building. It still exists in Gilbert Street. It was built in 1837 specifically for Mr Gouger, the first Colonial Secretary, for his own residence, and Mrs Gouger having died there was buried in the garden, but the body was later transferred to the cemetery on West Terrace. The comfort of this house was tenfold greater than that of the former, but the rent was nearly double. It may be seen that the early colonial pioneers not only endured the few inconveniences which new arrivals now experience, but also suffered many other more serious hardships and evils which have long ceased to exist.

Next in importance to getting a house to live in is getting good and regular supplies of life's necessities. In 1838 I read in the colonial paper this ominous advertisement: 'Fall in Bread! – William Parcell, bread and biscuit baker, at the Gilles Arcade, begs to inform the inhabitants of Adelaide that he is now selling bread of a superior quality at sixteen-pence per quartern loaf, for cash only.' Fall in bread indeed! My first weekly baker's bill indicated a rise instead of a fall, as it amounted to over thirty-seven shillings for bread alone, in addition to a substantial sum for flour and puddings, &c. The price of indispensable articles of consumption at that time fluctuated greatly and was regulated chiefly by the laws of supply and demand. All flour came from the neighbouring colonies, and was ground partly from wheat, but also contained large quantities of cheap, weevil-infested maize and low-grade rice. The prices of this compound at some periods ranged from £60 to £80 per ton, and at others from £90 to £100. The highest figure which I, as agent ever obtained for Tasmanian flour was £110. This of course is but a small indication of the type of household expenses to which immigrants to this and no doubt to other very young colonies at the time were subjected.

Sudden and extreme fluctuations connected with the supply of food not only affect families, but sometimes even threaten disaster to small communities. Once, I believe, Mr Osmond Gilles saved the colony from much distress by delving into personal funds; and on another occasion temporary famine was averted by Captain Duff, a very early and resourceful colonist, who, like most of the pioneers, has disappeared from our midst. The emigration commissioners in England had made no arrangement for the supply of meat to the settlement, and the stock on hand was nearly exhausted. In this emergency Captain Duff volunteered to take his vessel to Tasmania and get sheep. Some of the Government officers on their own authority pledged the Government to payment, but the guarantee of payment was not considered to be sound enough for Tasmanian merchants, and had Mr Duff's own mercantile credit not been good in the Van Diemen's Land market he would have had to return without a supply. He paid what portion of the bill he could with his own money, and made himself personally responsible for the remaining amount. But for this noble conduct the anxious colonists instead of being supplied with fat sheep would have felt exceedingly sheepish on Captain Duff's return. Shortly after that Mr Eyre arrived with 1000 sheep and 600 head of cattle; Captain Hart with 400 cattle; Dr Finlay with 600 sheep and 40 cattle; Mr Watson with 900 cattle; and Mr McFarlane with 1000 animals. There was no longer any fear of starvation. Duff's generous and somewhat imprudent action was forgotten with all possible haste. Rump steaks and other choice cuts of mutton were readily attainable for months to come. From this point onwards the arrival of stock was frequent and continuous, so much so, that at length sheep became valued mainly for their wool. Joints of mutton could then be had for 6d. each; heads and plucks were given away, chiefly to dogs and fowls; and thousands of sheep were boiled down for their fat.

Both skilled and unskilled labourers earned large sums of money in the early stages of the colony; and men who had never laboured before earned very large sums if they chose to doff their coats and go to work. But the improvidence of many working men, especially overlanders, was astonishing. Shepherds, station men, woodcutters, carters, and others similarly employed would work till a large sum was due, then go to the nearest township to spend it. The less imprudent of these were accustomed when the larger notes had vanished, to place the residue in the hands of a publican with instructions that he be notified when the money was nearly gone. Some would call for a dozen bottles of champagne, treat all hands present in tumblers, and break the glasses afterwards so as to have the pleasure of paying for them. Others who had received banknotes on partnership accounts, were to be seen, after some heavy drinking, dealing out the notes like cards from a pack, an equal number to each man, regardless of mixed denominations of tens, fives or ones.

I remember one worthy gentleman who chose Gawler as the locality for his spree. He was a woodcutter at the back of the township, and during his holiday, which lasted three days, got through nearly £50. Being informed on the morning of the fourth day that only £7 remained, and being heartily tired, probably of ceaseless drinking, and conscious that he could not tear himself away while the money remained, he shouted the bar until the amount was reduced to £5. 1s. 6d. He then paid 1s. 6d. for a pound of butter, and embedding a £5 note in it, threw it to his dog, who probably sustained indigestion from the extraordinary richness of his meal. The woodcutter then shouldered his swag and departed, much relieved both in mind and pocket.

I will mention one other instance. I knew one of the shepherds employed by the South Australian Company, who had been in their service for many years. The Manager told me that he was trustworthy and harmless at all times. He indulged in no luxury throughout the year except his stipulated allowance of tobacco; but when the annual pay-day came he received his wages, gave his receipt, proceeded to Adelaide, purchased his year's supply of clothing, then after having at length expended the balance of his wages on having a wild time, returned in the most orderly way to commence his next year's duties. No man could live a more regular life than that.

While writing of dwelling houses, I made no mention of public buildings. The Government Offices consisted mostly of weatherboards, scattered over different parts of the forest, as though some special advantage were obtainable through their being widely separated. The Post-Office was at the corner of North Terrace and King William Street, the Treasury and the Supreme Court were in Gilles Arcade, while the Government Store and some other offices were in the Park Lands. The site of the viceregal residence was close to the present Government House. When I first landed in South Australia I carried with me Government dispatches addressed to the Governor, Colonel

Gawler, so on arrival I reported without delay to His Excellency. I found Colonel Gawler kind, courteous, and communicative. Among other things he told me that the population of the colony – men, women, and children – was either one or two above or one or two below 5000. He added, with a significant smile, 'We have not yet found it necessary to take a census.'

Government House was an extraordinarily uncouth and repulsive structure. Its walls were of limestone and the roof of thatch. It resembled a moderately large barn which seemed as if it had been designed to violently contrast with the tall ugly external chimney. This interesting architectural peculiarity, His Excellency explained to me, had been erected by the party of marines who accompanied the first Governor, Captain Hindmarsh. The men, who by occupation spent much of their time at sea, obviously forgot that chimneys are so often a handy accessory on land built structures. A chimney was subsequently erected outside the wall and an aperture made in the masonry to connect one to the other. At a later date I witnessed the destruction of this primitive place by fire. The building was no loss, but unfortunately official documents contained in adjoining offices were consumed. The colony seemed subject to tragedies of this kind. Colonel Light's house at Thebarton had previously been burned to the ground, and with it papers relating to the origin and very early history of the province were destroyed. The residence of Mr John Brown of East Terrace met a like fate shortly afterwards and involved similar consequences. Thus the destruction of the old Government Offices was the third catastrophe of the kind.

One evening in January, 1841, I noticed from my house in Gilbert Street flames proceeding apparently from the neighbourhood of Government House. I was not long in reaching the spot, and, on arrival, found the frail walls and reed thatched roof of the old viceregal residence well ablaze. A large portion of the population had collected, and policemen and others were doing their best, but evidently ineffectually, to subdue the flames. Colonel Gawler was superintending the proceedings, and he several times ordered men to desist from placing their lives in peril by efforts which must necessarily have proved unavailing. He was perfectly calm, but nevertheless was evidently anxious and somewhat distressed. His chief regret was, of course, the wholesale destruction of official documents. My impression at the time was that these official statistics had from time to time been accumulated in the old office and never removed; but some persons asserted through the Press that the documents had been transferred to the recently built and more secure Government residence. They had temporarily been carried back to their old locality in order to furnish accommodation for Lady Franklin, who had visited South Australia to give directions for the erection at Port Lincoln of a memorial of her husband's arrival there with Flinders in November, 1802. Of this I shall have something to relate hereafter. Whatever may be the true version of the case I know not, but it is certain that the official documents were in the old hut at the time of the fire, and that their destruction was complete.

When the excitement had somewhat abated, I asked Colonel Gawler if he had any idea as to the origin of the fire. He replied, in his deliberate emphatic way, looking meanwhile expressively at the face of a person standing by whose expression I had previously observed contrasted with all other faces in the crowd by exhibiting a smile of apparent satisfaction. 'Unfortunately there is reason to believe that it is the work of an arsonist'. The Governor had at one time given offence to this man whose name I was later informed was McPherson. He was a very eccentric individual, and there was little doubt according to public opinion, as to his guilt in setting the fire. He was subsequently placed under temporary restraint and charged with being a lunatic. The jury however were unable to agree in their verdict. He was then remanded on a charge of arson but later set free, for there was no direct evidence to connect him with the destruction of the old Government Barn.

episode

IV

South Australian Register 30 January 1878

A TRANSPLANTED
VILLAGE

As already indicated, when I arrived in March, 1839, no rain had fallen for several months, so that the Park Lands and adjacent hills were quite bare in some parts, and nearly so in other places, the result being varying shades of brown vegetation and browner sterility. One's eye longed to rest on something more decidedly green than the narrow pointed leaves of the gum trees and wattles, or the not-so-graceful foliage of the she-oak. This yearning was sometimes gratified to some extent by the sight of a few cabbages, watermelons, or turnips and radishes, the green tops of which were perhaps more attractive to the eye than the taste of the roots were to the palate. These rarities were offered at almost prohibitive prices – cabbages, for instance, at from 2s. to 3s. each, and other items in proportion. The sellers were usually robust women or slender girls with their hair turned over their heads for a covering, dressed in woollen gowns in a huge variety of colours, and wearing clean striped aprons extending to just a little below the knees, and usually leaving the ankles bare. Their knowledge of the English language was limited almost to the names of the vegetables in which they dealt and of the coins received in payment. On enquiry I was informed that they were natives of Prussia: that they and their townspeople had left their native land on account of religious persecution; and that they had with the assistance of Mr George Fife Angas collectively emigrated to a place on the banks of the River Torrens. Along with themselves they imported the name of their village – 'Klemzig'. They were a small but compact and well-assorted community, comprising pastor, physician, tradesmen, agriculturists, horticulturists, and people of all needful occupations.

There was a degree of novelty in this mode of colonisation. I have of course witnessed the establishment of numerous towns and villages in this country, but they generally owe their existence to causes widely different from those that led to the foundation of Klemzig. Sometimes a patch of bush becomes a township by slow and gradual transition. The first step towards settlement is often made by a farmer who may take up a section at a distance from any township. If there happens to be a good supply of water at the place teamsters and travellers probably call, and as they require meals &c., a public house is in due time started, and various tradesmen follow. By-and-by a Post-Office is established, and thus the nucleus of a possibly, very important town exists. A township may also owe its foundation to a good bay or to the discovery of minerals, or again, to a rural property being laid out and sold in allotments by an enterprising speculator, and in these cases the progress of the settlement is often far more rapid than in the instance first named. But Klemzig was altogether an exception to any of the processes named. It most resembled a piece of the old country scooped out, conveyed across the ocean, and inserted in the soil of the new colony, in the same manner as forest trees, whole and growing, have been occasionally removed from one locality to another. I felt curious to visit this erratic fragment of continental Europe. I was informed that it was about three miles from North Adelaide, but in actual fact I found it further; and as the river ran through a forest in which innumerable paths had been worn, many of which seemingly leading to no place in particular it was easy for a stranger to lengthen his journey indefinitely. I started early on an intensely hot afternoon, and as I was accompanied by my family, several small pairs of legs began to feel somewhat weary after little more than an hour's walk. For some time, however, the novelty of the sundry blue, white, and yellow flowers in the pathway, and whole legions of cockatoos, parrots and other birds in the branches overhead tended to forestall complete fatigue. Nevertheless, seeing no signs of the German village and having quite lost our bearings, we at length sat down beside a little lake in the bed of the Torrens almost determined when rested to seek our way back to Adelaide. We had crossed the river more than once, and did not know with certainty on which side we were. This statement may appear strange to those who have only seen the Torrens as it is now [1878]; but at that time the river, like many Australian streams, became a series of lakes in dry weather, connected by rivulets, which in some places were very narrow, and in others quite shallow, but which always ran briskly. Thus instead of crossing the river once, we had unknowingly done so three or four times. We began to despair of reaching Klemzig, and naturally felt disappointed, as we had hoped to have obtained refreshment from the friendly Germans, and to have retraced our steps in the cool of the evening. Whilst considering the folly of continuing our excursion, I saw smoke rising above the tree-tops about a quarter of a mile ahead, and guessed that it must have been from the village chimneys.

We went forward in the direction thus indicated, and were very pleased on catching our first glimpse of Klemzig. It extended along the bank of the river for perhaps a third of a mile. The buildings consisted of earthen walls, newly white-washed, and straw-thatched roofs. Gardens with rich black mould, small but in excellent order, lay between the cottages and the river, and healthy vines and fruit-trees already gave

promise for the future; while enormous melons and vegetables
in abundance testified to the industry of the residents. At the
back of the line of cottages furthest from the river were fields
of stubble, and here and there might be seen the larger boys
and girls with sticks, beating the grain from heaps of wheat.
A few horses and cows were feeding, and numerous fowls
were going to roost in the gumtrees. We felt as if we were in
Germany instead of Australia. About the centre of the village
was a church, with white walls and thatched roof like the
other buildings. It was distinguishable by its somewhat larger
size and the form of the door, but more especially by the small
tower, within which was a bell. We entered and found it to be
in use as a school. The day's studies were just being finished.
Mr Kavel, the pastor, was teaching some dozen male urchins
and his wife a similar number of females. These disappeared
without hesitation as soon as permission to do so was given.
After some interesting conversation with the pastor and his wife
we were introduced to the Leader of the community, and then
made a tour of inspection throughout the village, the inhabitants
appearing at their doors or garden-gates with words and smiles
of welcome. Some of the words spoken were unintelligible to
us, but the smiles were genuine, and impossible to misinterpret.
At length we reached a house more lofty and spacious than
the general buildings. This we found to be the inn, the owner
of which, whose name was painted over the doorway, was the
moneyed man of the village. Although he had laid in no stock
of wines or beer he contrived to make us very comfortable. The
courteous civility with which every article of refreshment was
produced made it seem even more appealing and flavoursome,
though that was scarcely needed, as exercise and absence of
food and drink since morning had already made us extremely
hungry and most appreciative of any refreshment whatsoever.
We were supplied with freshly baked bread, cheese, fresh butter,

eggs, cream, milk, radishes, cress, &c., as well as excellent tea and coffee. Not content with having provided us all a plentiful meal, for which a very moderate sum was asked, we were laden, for our homeward journey, with spoils from both dairy and garden.

This trivial but pleasant incident occurred more than thirty-eight years ago. I was over at the site of Klemzig some years later and found myself among ruins. The river, which at that spot is very picturesque, remained unaltered, yet it seemed to glide along more gloomily than before past the decaying habitations encumbering its bank. Most of the cottages were uninhabited. The whitewash had peeled off in large flakes from the walls, and the dirty strips which remained served only to give the crumbling mud a yet more desolate appearance. There is, however, no need to be regretfully sentimental over this for I am told that this is the only 'deserted village' in the colony. The causes that led to its desertion are the exact opposite to those that are known to have depopulated towns and villages throughout the world. The thrifty, hard-working villagers, having during the terms of their leases amassed sufficient savings from their farms to secure much larger holdings, subsequently most bought sections of their own, mostly, I believe, near Hahndorf and Lobethal and in other hilly districts, where their agriculture and horticultural pursuits have been successful and useful both to themselves and to the colony. Of course now, after the lapse of thirty-eight years, many of the founders of Klemzig are dead; but their descendants may be found throughout the entire colony.

episode

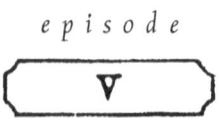

South Australian Register 6 February 1878

MY FIRST ACQUAINTANCE WITH NATIVES

One of the strangest and most startling sensations which, despite all that may have been previously read and heard on that subject, is experienced by a small white community on settling amid a large population of Australian aborigines. This arises from the extreme contrast of both colour and culture between the two races. A short period, however, is all that is required to narrow the margin between these differences, for the darker race speedily falls into a new lifestyle, though for them it is a false or at least an abnormal one. It has lost none of the vices of barbarism, and has probably gained the coarser vices of civilisation, previously unknown. It is a lamentable fact, to which I can bear personal testimony, that in the early stages of South Australian history men, most of whom were convicts from neighbouring colonies, worked energetically and perseveringly to corrupt the natives, and succeeded to a great extent in counteracting agencies of an opposite nature instituted by the Governor and many philanthropic settlers. It is a curious and painful problem why aboriginal races almost invariably disappear comparatively soon after the arrival of dominant and Christianised communities. That they do so diminish is undoubtedly the fact. Where are the Indian tribes of North and South America with which the British and Spaniards first came in contact? Many of them are extinct, and many others nearly so. Where, too, will the semi-civilised and once powerful population of New Zealand be half a century hence? Judging from present appearances, the race will doubtless have given place, chiefly through conquest and partly through amalgamation, to the encroaching and absorbing Anglo-Saxon. The South Sea Islanders will no doubt similarly disappear. The formerly numerous natives of Tasmania are entirely extinct, and of those of New South Wales and Victoria only inconsiderable remnants remain. To come nearer home, many South Australian tribes which were numerous and strong within my own recollection have either entirely died out or have but one or two representatives left. In too many instances these are half-castes, or have been transformed into anomalous semblances of 'white-fellows', reflecting unfortunately no credit on any human colour. Even though barbarity may account for the extinction of South American tribes, or continual conflict for the diminution of the North American Indians, still these causes will not avail to explain the disappearance of those of South Australia. We have had some smart brushes with them at the Rufus, Port Lincoln, and a few other places, but these have been rare exceptions. Where the rifle and sword are not the agents of extermination, aboriginal tribes appear nevertheless to melt away of themselves. As far as they are concerned, 'Who fights finds death, and death finds him who flies.'

There were no natives on the Park Lands of Adelaide when I first walked up from Glenelg, and the few that I saw at Holdfast Bay on landing were picked men, who aided the Europeans on arrival of a vessel. Natives with their domestic surroundings were to me still an unsolved problem. At dusk of an evening at the latter end of April, or it might be early in May 1839, I observed several fires springing up on the northern side of the Torrens. This I knew indicated a native embranchment, for to call it an encampment would be a misnomer. The night was moonless, the sky was mottled with streaks of clouds and starry patches between. Some fifty or sixty fires, duly reflected from above, and mingling with, almost quenching, the stellar rays, so illuminated the branches of the noble gum-trees which then fringed the river that it is probable all parrots, opossums, and other tenants having vested interest in the said trees had temporarily removed to the then rural districts of Klemzig, Walkerville, Kensington, or Unley. Amid the lurid glare and smoke arising from the fires flitted here and there black garbless figures, streaked and spotted with white, red and yellow daubs. The whole scene combined with accompanying sounds, furnished a most eligible idea of a thoroughly legitimate and respectable pandemonium.

The sounds already alluded to consisted of an unearthly and wailing sort of chant, in which the voices of men, women, and children were distinctly and separately perceptible, sometimes one and sometimes another becoming predominant. The voices were accompanied by a dull beating sound, produced by the open hand, or by sticks struck against the blankets or skin garments of the performers, the said garments being spread on the ground before them. The precision with which time was kept perfectly astonished me. The whole affair produced in my mind the idea of something that I have before described as unearthly. The strangely mingled light and the strangely blended sounds were so unlike the gaslight and rumbling of vehicles in European cities that I felt as if under the wand of enchantment. Presently harlequin-coloured forms arranged themselves in combined or opposing masses for sham battles, or war dances, or, to use their own term, for 'corroboree'. I determined on a nearer inspection, and the season being one of drought I proceeded westward to that part of the river where Horton James, in his book, *Six months in South Australia* claimed to have stepped across it without being aware of the fact that it consisted of water. There I jumped over. I proceeded nearly to the spot where the sable gymnastics were being carried on by the Murray and other distant tribes, when, blinded to objects near at hand by fires glaring in every direction around me, my foot struck against something of considerable solidity, which answered the kick with a gruff and emphatic 'hoo!' On looking down I discovered the object to be - not a burnt stump, which of course would not have uttered such an exclamation, but a human head chiselled in ebony. Several other owners of heads as well as the kickee, who were lying about awaiting their turn in the corroboree - their large, liquid, black eyes glistening the while like stars of the wrong colour - started up on all sides of me unclothed, and regularly besieged me with appeals, not in their musical vernacular, but in such barbarous hybrid phrases as the following: 'Hallo, Williamy.' 'What namee you?' 'My name Bole.' 'Div me whitey money.' 'Bickety, bread,' 'You barry goot shentleman; div me tixpence.' That was my first introduction to the Adelaide tribe.

With a piece of silver I gladly compensated for the assault, and having spent an hour or so in witnessing the strange festivities retired with sensations of a mingled nature, in which the painful undoubtedly predominated. The chief cause of that pain was the evident degradation from Stone-Age simplicity to repulsive vice which the Adelaide tribe had undergone through contact with my countrymen. Paying the latter, as well as myself an ill compliment, I designated them 'Anglified natives'. In a future chapter, under the title 'Primitive natives', I shall have an opportunity of describing tribes in the Far West, which when I resided among them had not been brought within the contaminating influence of Europeans.

The position in which I beheld the Adelaide tribe that night was similar to that of all other tribes after white men have settled on their hunting-grounds. A defined quantity of land which they had roamed over from time immemorial was their own especial inheritance, as distinguished from districts belonging to other tribes. Not possessing the white man's knowledge, they had failed to put the land to its most profitable uses, but without hindrance or molestation they had sated their hunger with the flesh of wild quadrupeds and birds which roamed over it, and with roots indigenous to the soil. The former were now scared away, and the latter to a great extent eradicated to make room for the white man's sheep, wheat and potatoes. Driven over the boundaries of other tribes, the trespassers were of course forcibly repelled. The more distant savages were not so abundantly endowed with game and esculents as to be able to share them with dispossessed neighbours. Thus they had necessarily become pensioners, relying on the bounty of those who had possessed themselves of and overrun their wild hereditary lands. Of course flour and blankets were forthcoming from the Government at stated times. Benevolent individuals – both official and non-official – sought to counteract the adverse influences which were operating against them, but only with partial effect. Private benevolence in such cases is too often exercised without judgment. One individual will give a native food or money without requiring an equivalent; another will employ a strong man all day, say in procuring and cutting firewood, and in the evening furnish him with food scarcely sufficient for his own supper, while perhaps at his branchy sheltering-place members of his family are waiting to share his earnings; while another, in return for a slight service which occupied a few minutes, bestows a coin which will provide ample food for a day or two. With such a system, or rather want of it, where can the utterly uninformed native find an incentive to industry? How can he possibly become aware of the value of his labour? As far as Adelaide is concerned this is a matter of the past; but incidents that occurred here thirty-eight years ago are repeating themselves in other parts of the continent. Is it surprising that these roaming and resourceless tribes should, under such altered circumstances, gradually dwindle and at length disappear? Their accustomed mode of life is rendered impracticable; their ordinary supplies of food are unobtainable; they are brought under the operation of laws which they do not comprehend; and the customs or laws to which they were born they are not permitted to practise and enforce. Unskilled in any kinds of labour but those required for the chase or battle, they necessarily become helplessly dependent. To these causes of impairment the more baneful ones already alluded to having been added, it cannot be wondered at that the majority of the Adelaide tribe at the period of which I write had become dirty, abject, whining beggars.

It is now a rare occurrence to see a group of natives or even an isolated individual, in the more settled districts. I doubt if a single member of the Adelaide tribe, or of any tribe in the immediate neighbourhood, could now be produced. Where are the tribes and families that thirty-eight years ago were distributed over the whole of our now settled districts? They have not been absorbed by the white population either as servants or otherwise. They have not amalgamated with tribes beyond the settled districts, that is certain. Where are they?

episode

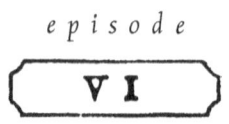

South Australian Register 13 February 1878

FIRST GLIMPSES OF THE BUSH

During the first few months of my residence in the colony the immediate suburbs of Adelaide had but partially resigned their bush characteristics. It was not only possible but easy to lose oneself in the daytime in almost any direction at the distance of only a few miles. Wallabies, wild turkeys, snakes, and dingoes would present themselves to the equestrian or pedestrian traveller, gaze with astonishment at him and at the innovations which were being made on their ancient domain, and instantly bound, stride, or glide, according to their several tastes and habits, back into the neighbouring wilderness – that is, if permitted to do so by the unscrupulous innovator.

My first trip of any length was to Gawler. The distance from Adelaide by rail is twenty-five miles. But of course in 1839 there was no railway by which to travel. How many miles were stepped by my horse's hoofs I am unable to say – probably thirty-five. At that time no habitation had been erected between North Adelaide and the town which was honoured with the name of our second Governor. It consisted then of three thatched cottages, one of which was the little inn afterwards designated the 'Old Spot'. How quickly does the word 'old' come into use even in a juvenile community!

I have with much satisfaction made the Old Spot my

resting place several scores of times since that name has been conferred on it, but never has it yielded me such enjoyment as when in its babyhood I arrived sunburnt, dusty, and thirsty at the shade of its humble verandah, and beheld its white tablecloth and the long-awaited refreshments which instantly made their appearance thereon.

From Adelaide to Gawler, or vice versa, was at that time a disagreeable ride in extremely hot weather. The wayfarer traversed an open plain on which no human habitation had been erected between the two townships. To meet, overtake, or be overtaken by another traveller was a rare occurrence. In cool moist weather, when a grassy carpet variegated with flowers of diversified hues more gracefully distributed than could have been suggested by the most skilful designer of patterns was spread beneath you, the ride was pleasant enough. Then an emu, a kangaroo, but more frequently a bustard or two, would cross your path, and instantly retreat amid the belt of trees which continuously intervened between the apparently interminable plain and the shore of St Vincent's Gulf; and drinkable water could be found at convenient intervals. But when the soil was bare and dusty, and unveiled sun, scorching from above, and water was only obtainable at distant intervals, the ride was somewhat trying.

Most of my early journeys there occurred under such circumstances. On my sixth or seventh visit, on reaching the Little Para I was pleased to observe a dray on the southern side of the river, with a draught horse tethered and feeding not far away. Some ambulatory dealer, thought I, camping here until the sun has descended lower. I had a sandwich in my saddle-bag, and a pannikin wherewith to transfer a portion of the limpid current of the Para to my lips, for at that spot I intended to halt, as I had done on previous journeys. I had just dismounted when an individual whom I knew (everybody knew everybody then) emerged from beneath the shade of a tarpaulin and bade me welcome. Within two minutes something white – it was too small for a tablecloth – was placed on a packing-case; a York ham, boiled and not materially encroached on as to substance, a bottle of pickles, a crusty loaf, and butter which, thanks to the streamlet which was gurgling by, was solid as a splinter of rock, were duly arranged on the impromptu tablecloth. I was invited to help myself, but thirst in my case having for the moment the ascendancy over hunger, I stooped to the current, and was about to fill my pannikin with the limpid element, when the host exclaimed – 'Stop!' Producing with either hand, from a couple of casks whose lower ends were luxuriating in the margin of the current while their heads were covered with a liberal supply of cold wet straw, a bottle, whose head was instantly knocked off with the back of a carving knife, he began to pour from both simultaneously, in bush fashion, into my pannikin. A considerable liquid commotion ensued, which terminated in a friendly combination of Burton ale and London stout, which my kind host denominated 'half and half'. Hitherto, I had always enjoyed a draught of Para, but I must express my belief that on that particular occasion, considering the heated state of my blood, I derived more benefit therefrom than I should have done from cold water neat. This little 'fixing', as our American cousins would call it, was the prelude to a small inn which shortly after made its appearance close to the spot, which gradually expanded into a comfortable hotel. It was initially called the 'Stock Keeper Inn', but some time later it too became known as the Old Spot. I have no doubt that it continues to prosper, although a greedy railway absorbs the lion's share of traffic in that direction.

 On the hill at the northern extremity of what is now Murray Street, and where a much used graveyard has long existed, there was just a solitary mound in the year 1839, which for me possessed some interest. It was unenclosed and without a gravestone or other indication of its nature. As if the sod resented the violence done to its primeval repose the native grasses were already creeping over it and in part obliterating the contrast of colour which alone distinguished it from the neighbouring herbage. It was, I believe, the first grave dug in that part of the country, and contained the body of one of my fellow passengers named Pratt. He was a young man of considerable talent, an amateur artist, and had wandered to the banks of the River Gawler to sketch the magnificent scenery, water, and woodland that then distinguished the spot. Not returning from his artistic tour, he was of course searched for, and after the lapse of two or three days was discovered lifeless on the mossy base of a remarkable large and symmetrical gumtree. It was evident that he had died in a sitting posture. Beside him, were his portfolio and wallet. His sandwich dinner was untouched. At his feet lay the pencil that no doubt he was in the act of using when his spirit flitted to far different scenes. Near it was the half-finished sketch of a noble and peculiarly marked giant of the forest. He was known to have been affected by disease of the heart, which fact, and the circumstances in which he was found, clearly indicated the cause of his death. Shortly after the period of which I write, shipmates of the deceased, finding that his unprotected grave was occasionally molested by wild dogs, paid for a railing to be placed around it.

My next journey was a longer one and in the opposite direction – to Encounter Bay. We then called the distance sixty miles. No visible road existed. Colonel Gawler had caused trees to be notched as a guide for several miles, but there was still great possibility of losing the road. The latter half of the journey had to be effected over or through loose sand and repulsive scrub. A glimpse of the colony's most sterile territory was then obtained.

Very different was the impression produced by scenery

between Adelaide and Mount Barker. The ascent of hill after hill over fertile soil, amid majestic trees, thickly scattered flowers, birds in abundance, and fanned by cool and fragrant breezes, had something exhilarating in it. Then glances backward over the apparently diminutive plain and City of Adelaide to the open sea and around as far as eye could reach, and glances downwards at intervals into gullies choked with vegetation and ravines descending almost perpendicularly to such depths that objects of fair dimensions at the bottom were dwarfed almost beyond identification – scenes such as these convinced the traveller that he had arrived in a country by no means deficient in beauty or picturesqueness. On return from my first journey to Mount Barker, the night being dark, I lost my way among the hills, tethered my horse, and having rolled into my blanket, lay beside a tree until daylight. In the morning I was somewhat startled to find that I was within a very few feet of the edge of a precipice, which for a considerable distance had a sheer descent. Had I during the night been aware of my exact position I should not have slept so soundly and comfortably as I did.

What a beautiful bit of fairy ground, when I first saw it in 1840, was the section of land on which Burnside now stands! I had walked from Adelaide one hot summer day, leaving Kensington, one of the earliest suburban townships, on my left, and followed the course of the creek towards the hills. The creek guided me into a natural shrubbery, the shade of which was most inviting. After crossing the road to Glen Osmond, the creek separated for a short space into two currents and then reunited, forming thereby a delightful little island. On this, a temporary Robinson Crusoe, I took rest for some time plucking wild flowers, listening to a chorus of small birds, and watching innumerable little yabbies as they darted about among the white and brown pebbles which formed the bottom of the stream.

EPISODE VI

After a sufficient pause I proceeded upwards, when I perceived a man without coat or waistcoat bending over the stream. I had not seen an individual during the last two miles of my walk, and did not expect to find one here. 'Somebody catching crayfish,' said I to myself. He did not perceive my approach until I was close to him. When he assumed an erect posture I recognised in him a frequent customer of mine for damaged grain, coarse sugar, and such like commodities. I often wondered what he did with the rubbish he bought. The supposition of a lolly manufactory would not fully satisfy my inquiring mind. For where was such an establishment located? Where also were the manufactured articles sold? And to whom? Looking into the creek, whose surface was rippling, yet nevertheless as transparent as crystal, I beheld the worm of a still. I laughed heartily, and he did the same. 'Don't stay staring there,' said he, 'come along here.' He preceded me to a shady little hut roofed with bark, which was scarcely discoverable among surrounding foliage. There he set before me hunter's beef, bread, butter, cheese, and a good-sized jug of something which had probably the year before been in my auction room in a state of solidity. A very small quantity of the rather powerful liquid sufficed, for there were many a hazard to be encountered by an unsteady foot between there and home.

Some years after the foregoing incident a gentleman bought from the South Australian Company the section which had been intermediately leased to another party, and placed it in my hands for subdivision as a township. Of course I immediately inspected the land with a view to mapping it out so that as many allotments as possible might benefit by the running water. With much surprise I perceived that since I first saw the section it had been cultivated and abandoned. European trees and shrubs were flourishing. But the altered condition of the spot will best be gathered from the advertisement that announced the auction:

Burnside the Beautiful — A.B. feels real pleasure in introducing to the notice of all who value health, fertility, and beauty, Preliminary Section No. 320, situated one mile above Kensington, at the foot of the most picturesque mountain of the whole magnificent range nearest Adelaide. Excellent roads surround the section on all sides. A clear and ever flowing stream meanders through it, producing luxuriant, diversified, and perennial vegetation. Amid the wattle and other native flowering shrubs appear (the result of cultivation in the 'olden time') the gorgeous rose, clinging honeysuckle, climbing clematis, the fragrant briar, geraniums in rich profusion, nasturtiums, sweet-peas, garden herbs of every species, a forest of Cape gooseberries, the wayward strawberry, figs, peaches, nectarines, vines of choicest varieties, apples, oranges, plums, almonds and pomegranates. Even the weeping willow inclines its graceful form and extends its swaying arms over the stream which has nurtured it since the foundation of the colony. New colonists will do well to become acquainted with a scene of beauty whose existence is unsuspected by most of them. The sea views are bounded only by the shore of the Gulf or the horizon, and the neighbouring walks are romantic in the extreme. The sale will take place — — —.

The foregoing inflated advertisement, elaborately displayed, produced the effect desired by announcers of auctions; it attracted public attention and drew a large crowd to the sale. The land was disposed of satisfactorily, and Burnside is now a populous as well as a pretty suburb of Adelaide.

episode

South Australian Register 20 February 1878

TWO WRECKS; THE FANNY AND MARIA

Any one who has resided among tribes of South Australian natives in their primitive conditions will have observed that Europeans on their first reception are met not with hostility but with friendliness. Those unhappy misunderstandings which too frequently follow the meeting occasioning outrage and retaliation having to be accounted for by incidents, known or unknown, in which, very often native women have borne some part. The reception of the earliest South Australian colonists by the tribes with which they first came in contact was of a friendly character, and has been put on record. The Editor of the *South Australian Gazette and Colonial Register* on June 3, 1837, published a small article titled 'The Natives', from which the following passage was taken:

> It is a source of much gratification to find that the natives of that portion of the province chosen for the first settlement are far superior to the ordinary race of New Hollanders. Their friendly disposition, honesty, and inoffensive conduct may fairly set at rest all the fears that might at first have been entertained.

The same characteristics belonged to the tribes located in the neighbourhood of Encounter Bay and the River Murray, as was proved by the experience of the crew and passengers of the wrecked schooner *Fanny* in June–August, 1838. The *Fanny* sailed from Tasmania, bound for Western Australia, having on board as passengers the Rev. Mr Longbottom, Wesleyan missionary, his wife and their little boy, who is now [1878] forty years older, and is greatly respected in Adelaide. By a gale of wind, or a very violent series of squalls, the vessel was driven ashore on our southern coast, not far from Cape Jaffa. All aboard waded ashore up to their necks in water, except the boy, who was borne through the surf by Captain Gill, master of the vessel. Mrs Longbottom was under water so long that she almost drowned, and required resuscitation.

On the forenoon of the day following the wreck nine natives visited the survivors, gave them the means of making a fire, showed them where to find fresh water, and rendered all assistance in their power. The Longbottom family was later moved to a temporary camp that had been set up on Captain Gill's instructions, near some lagoons. They remained here for several weeks while the Captain and several of his crew, through great feats of endurance, managed to reach Encounter Bay, where they sent word to Adelaide advising of the disaster. Captain Gill then returned to the camp with a small rescue party in a whaleboat. The Longbottom family and the remainder of the crew from the *Fanny* were, after several futile attempts, delivered safely to Adelaide where Mr Longbottom later decided to settle in his ministerial capacity, abandoning his original intention of proceeding to King George's Sound. During the whole time they were stranded and awaiting rescue, they experienced uniform kindness from the local tribes, of whom Captain Gill in the concluding passages of his official report stated: 'They are, most decidedly, the most inoffensive race I ever met.'

Let us pass on to the wreck of the *Maria*, which occurred within two years of the former disaster at no great distance from the

EPISODE VII

same spot. All on board that ill-fated brigantine perished – not by the sea, but by natives. It so chanced that some of my fellow voyagers from England were among the murdered persons. Two of them were Mr James York and his wife. That respectable couple commenced their colonial life at Kensington, one of the earlier established suburbs of Adelaide. There they built and furnished a comfortable cottage, and apparently had made South Australia their home; but from circumstances which Mr York explained to me, and which now escape my memory, they determined to move to Tasmania.

The *Maria*, a vessel of about 130 tons, arrived at Port Adelaide on 7th June, 1840 from Hobart Town, and sailed from the same port in ballast exactly two weeks later. The Yorks booked passage on the *Maria*, and hurriedly disposed of their property in this colony. Satisfactory prices were obtained by auction, and they received the net proceeds in gold, which accounts for the number of sovereigns which, after the murders, were found in the possession of the natives, or at the whalefishery at Encounter Bay, where the natives had no doubt taken them. Toward the end of the month news arrived in Adelaide from Encounter Bay that several white people, who had probably escaped from some wreck upon the coast, had been murdered by natives in the neighbourhood of Rivoli Bay. Their number was stated to be between twenty and thirty, inclusive of men, women, and children. On receipt of this distressing intelligence Mr Pullen (now Admiral Pullen), who was then stationed at Goolwa, was instructed to organise a party, proceed up the Coorong in a whaleboat, and ascertain the extent and details of the tragedy. This was promptly done, and on 30th July, on one of the shores of the Coorong, the party discovered separate limbs and other portions of several human bodies, horribly bruised and mutilated and divested of all clothing, the latter having evidently been carried away. As nearly as could be calculated these ghastly remains had partly constituted two men, three women, and four children. Wedding rings had been removed from the fingers of two of the women. The remainder of the day was spent in committing these human fragments to the ground.

Next day the party continued their search up the Coorong. Most of the natives who approached within sight betrayed conscious fear and skulked among the scrub; a few, however, after a time ventured to hold conversation with the occupants of the boat. From them information was obtained that the shipwrecked people had unwisely separated into independent groups and pursued different routes. By so doing of course they afforded to the murderers an opportunity of dispatching them in detail. Many natives were now seen clad more or less in European garments. One very affecting incident occurred during this part of the search. In the moist soil of the side of the Coorong were discerned the tracks of Europeans, including those of children. At a short distance the latter disappeared, while those of the adults were continued, a probable indication that the little ones had become tired and were carried onwards by their parents.

On these horrible and indisputable facts becoming generally known in Adelaide the whole population including the Governor, Colonel Gawler, became convinced that the Government must take very decisive action – that aboriginal tribes, however numerous, formidable and warlike, or rather for those very reasons, must be taught that the invincible power of the white man would, in the event of them committing such atrocities, visit them with prompt and adequate punishment. In fact it had become apparent that those South-eastern tribes required an unequivocal and permanent lesson – and they had it. A strong body of mounted police was mustered and dispatched to the scene of the atrocities under the command of Commissioner, Major O'Halloran, who was accompanied by

Inspector Tolmer. A body of volunteers scarcely less numerous, who were commanded by Mr Bonny, supported his force. I was not a member of the latter force, but showed my support on the occasion by lending my horse to a volunteer who did not possess one. Prior to their departure the party drew up in front of Government House, and Colonel Gawler conversed for a few minutes with the Major. Two or three minutes later the volunteers commenced their march, and the Governor spoke in complimentary terms of them in regard to their serviceable appearance and military bearing. When the march commenced the crowd cheered heartily and Colonel Gawler, commenting on the police contingent, remarked, 'That is a very fine body of men.' The Commissioner himself was also very proud of them. On a subsequent occasion at Port Lincoln, where he had gone on another dramatic and melancholy mission, he said to me, 'I believe every man under me is a gentleman, for whenever I discover one of them to be a blackguard he is immediately dismissed.'

On their arrival at the scene of the murders the combined force created great consternation among the natives, who had assembled in hundreds. Most of them possessed some garment or shred of European clothing. In many instances these were stained, and in some absolutely drenched with blood. In the latter instances the upper portions of the garments were most discoloured – a fact which seems to confirm statements made by native women that most of the victims were held by natives while others battered their heads with clubs. Besides wearing apparel the horsemen found two watches, the dial of one of them being stained with blood, part of a bible, several other books, newspapers, letters more or less torn, some silver spoons, and part of the log of the *Maria*. They discovered other bodies, which as to their mutilated condition resembled those which had been found by Mr Pullen's party. The group of bodies first discovered

I do not doubt were those of Mr and Mrs York, Mr and Mrs Denham, the majority of their children, and another female. The wedding rings taken from the bodies were afterwards identified as those of Mrs Denham and Mrs York.

The Denhams had five children with them, and the Yorks one, an infant, but not all could be accounted for among the bodies discovered. Mr Denham and Mrs York were brother and sister. The total number of passengers on board the *Maria* was sixteen, and the ship's company, including Captain Smith and his mate, numbered ten, and of those twenty-six souls, not an individual survived the slaughter.

When the well-armed troopers and their allies, the volunteers, galloped into the midst of the congregated natives, an indescribable scene of terror and confusion ensued. They were hunted through the scrub on all sides, and sought refuge in all sorts of impractical places; some took to the water, and some were driven into reedy morasses. Between fifty and sixty, the majority of whom were women and children, were temporarily secured as prisoners. That many casualties must incidentally have occurred among them during that extensive and protracted hunt is probable; but the only deaths deliberately inflicted were reported to be four. Two men pointed out by other natives as murderers were shot while running away, and another two, convicted by a sort of martial law, were suspended from branches of trees over the graves of some of the murdered people. In accordance with English law that permitted the use of gibbets, the bodies were left dangling as a warning to remaining tribesmen. The tribes were told not to remove them, and they reverently obeyed the directive.

A great deal was said and written at the time about the legality of the proceedings. Strictly speaking they were not legal. No Judge and Jury authorised the executions. But there are cases of emergency wherein adherence to strict law would cause substantial injustice, and that was one of them. The terrible but needful punishment then inflicted on the blacks was an act of mercy towards them, and no doubt prevented the loss of many further lives.

episode

South Australian Register 28 February 1878

MURDER OF JOHN GOFTON

The murder of John Gofton north of Adelaide, near the mouth of the Para River, was perpetrated in July 1840. Great doubt prevailed in the public mind as to the perpetrator of the deed, although circumstantial evidence produced at the inquest, which occupied three days, was legally conclusive against Joseph Stagg. The Jury, two of whom, with the Coroner, inspected the body on the spot where it was found prior to its removal to Adelaide, returned a unanimous verdict of, 'Wilfully murdered by Joseph Stagg.' A bush journey by the other Jurymen was considered unnecessary.

In the following November Stagg was tried before Chief Justice Cooper, convicted, and on the 18th of that month executed, having to the last emphatically and persistently declared his innocence. That was one of the earliest executions of a white man that occurred in the colony. The first had been the result of an alarming attempt to commit murder, which fortunately failed to be successful. The attempt by Michael Magee to murder the Sheriff, Mr Samuel Smart, was made on 27 March, 1838, before my arrival in the colony.

Mr Smart was sitting in his office writing, when two men named Magee and Morgan entered the apartment unannounced. The former aimed a gun at the Sheriff, and fired, the lead shot grazed Mr Smart's ear and seared a mark on his cheek-bone which was still quite visible when I first met him a year later, and I believe it remained so for the rest of his life. The assailed official instantly rose, seized the gun and wrested it from Magee; but both the villains managed to escape. They were, however, speedily captured, convicted, and sentenced – Magee capitally, and Morgan to transportation for life. The execution took place on 2 May, 1838 on the North Park Lands, near to the Government's iron store; and the tree from one of whose branches the criminal was suspended was for years pointed out to any newcomer as a noteworthy object. The infliction of the sentence was terribly bungled. No executioner had previously been required, consequently none had been appointed, and now a volunteer to perform the repulsive task could not be found, although large sums were offered as a temptation. I believe, by law, if the Sheriff cannot find a substitute he is bound personally to carry the sentence into force. In this particular instance the Sheriff having been the party assailed, such a proceeding would have been peculiarly unseemly. Much speculation on the subject was hazarded on the fatal morning, but was dispelled when a cart was driven under the branch that had been selected as a gallows. In the cart was a coffin whereon sat two individuals, one being Michael Magee and the other an unknown person diabolically disguised, but which, even the youngest child present knew must be the executioner. Magee displayed great nerve throughout. In a clear voice he confessed his guilt, which had been made too clear for him to admit otherwise; but as men of this class must apparently solemnly deny something at the last moment of life, he emphatically denied that he was a 'runaway convict', as alleged at the trial. Perhaps he possessed a ticket of leave.

That the infant colony could not furnish an individual skilful in the art of hanging may be a credit to it, but certainly a melancholy tragedy ensued. When the cap had been drawn over the culprit's face, and the hempen noose, which dangled from the branch above, placed about his neck, the horses were whipped forward, but proceeded so deliberately he was left suspended with unbroken neck, the knot of the rope instead of being under his ear, being under his chin. The poor wretch managed to free his arms and held on with both hands to the rope which should have strangled him almost instantaneously, uttering meanwhile most heart-rendering cries for mercy. The hangman, who had absented himself, returned, and clinging to the dying man's legs completed his horrid work by main force.

The circumstances that proceeded the execution, of which I intend to speak more at length, were widely different from the foregoing. Goften and Stagg were two members of a gang of cattle stealers, most of whom were from Van Diemen's Land. Cattle that found their way into the possession of these men were held in secluded camps in the Mount Lofty Tiers [Ranges] or in the thickly wooded areas of the Black Forrest. At the appropriate time these beasts were converted into beef for secret home sales or for export. John Goften had been arrested on a charge of cattle stealing and committed to prison to await his trial. With the assistance of his accomplices he effected his escape, and for several weeks his whereabouts were unknown to the authorities. Extra care was taken by the police to ensure that he should not leave the colony by sea. At length, towards the end of July 1840, Inspector Tolmer and his constables discovered tracks that they believed had been made by Stagg and Gofton, near the mouth of the River Para. These guided them eventually to a hut in a mangrove swamp, on entering which they found Gofton lying on his back with arms extended and quite dead, death apparently having very recently occurred. A fire in the hut, near which probably the murdered man had been sitting a few hours before, had not quite died out. The cause of death was obvious, the charge of a gun having passed through his head from side to side. The body appeared to have been removed a few yards from where it had fallen. The coat of the deceased lay at some distance from it, and the sleeves were turned inside out. Twelve sovereigns and three half-sovereigns were found, also a canister of damp gunpowder and a few other articles of small value, which furnished no key to the mystery of Gofton's death. No firearms were found. Stagg was at once suspected, and promptly apprehended by Trooper J. B. Lomas.

The evidence adduced at the inquest was wholly circumstantial, as is usually the case when murder is the crime investigated. Its leading features were the following: Stagg was the closest intimate of Gofton, the last person seen in his company, and was believed to have planned his escape from prison. Immediately before the murder Stagg was seen riding from Adelaide towards the mouth of the Para armed with a gun; at a later hour that day [Sunday] two witnesses saw a man they firmly believed to be Stagg, riding rapidly back towards Adelaide, the gun being still in his possession. At a public house at Islington, about two miles distant from Adelaide, he took refreshment and rested his horse, which had the appearance of having been overworked; and no wonder, for Stagg was a heavy man, and he said he had ridden thirty miles since morning. At two o'clock that Sunday afternoon he was seen terminating his journey in Morphett Street. At four o'clock he rode from South Adelaide to North Adelaide on a fresh horse, with a gun on his arm. A witness proved that he had lent Stagg a horse on Saturday, which he received back from him on Sunday evening. The most damning evidence against Stagg was a pair of shoes of very peculiar make found in his house in Adelaide which fitted exactly into footprints impressed on soft earth near Gofton's hut. The position of the several indentations relative to each other was such as would ensue from the tread of a splay-footed man, which Stagg was. At first sight this fact appears conclusive, but as it was proved in evidence that Stagg had been in the neighbourhood of the hut thirty-six hours before the alleged Sunday visit, some doubt arises as to exactly when the footprints may, or may not have been made. It was certainly proven that he returned to Adelaide after visiting the Para on Friday and that he started in that direction again on Sunday morning. He attempted to prove an alibi for his whereabouts on Sunday, but totally failed.

I have not been able to peruse the evidence submitted at the trial, and was in Court only during a portion of its progress, but believe it to have been substantially the same as that before summarised. The doubt felt by many as to Stagg's guilt possessed some remarkable features. The evening before his execution Mr Charles Mann, his counsel, spent an hour or two at my cottage. His spirits were evidently greatly depressed. I started topics which I knew were of great interest to him, but without stimulating his customary enthusiasm. At length I queried him on his abstraction, to which he replied, 'A man is to be hanged to-morrow morning for a crime of which I know him to be innocent.' He then informed me of personal appeals that he had made to the Chief Justice and to the Governor, both without effect. The former of course discerned no reason for reversing the verdict of the Jury, and the latter would not exercise the royal prerogative of mercy without special grounds for doing so having been shown. I remarked to Mr Mann that in conversation with Stagg, whom I saw between his committal and his trial, while he emphatically asserted his innocence of killing Gofton he admitted that he had committed crimes even more heinous.

This observation provoked a very natural retort, enunciated in Mr Mann's most expressive tone – 'A man is not to be hanged for what he did not do, simply because he did something else for which he deserved hanging' – a legal and moral fact which of course I did not dispute.

In conversation with Chief Justice Cooper on the day of the execution, he confided in me by saying, 'I wish the evidence at the trial had been stronger on some points, however, I do not see that the Jury could have arrived at any other decision.' It was even more remarkable that Mr Ashton, Keeper of the Gaol, who for many years had been a member of England's famous Bow Street police establishment, and who might therefore be regarded as an expert in assessing the guilt or innocence of an individual, asserted until the day of his death his belief in the innocence of Stagg. He used to get almost angry when anyone announced a contrary opinion. He would say, 'He perpetrated many crimes, but he did not do that for which he died.' This is the more extraordinary because Stagg was very communicative, and even confidential in discussion with him. Among other atrocities which he revealed to Ashton was the following: In Tasmania he and others divested a woman of her clothing, secured her with stakes over a living nest of venomous ants, and left her to die a slow, horrid and torturous death – a diabolical act which alone merited, not a speedy and comparatively easy death, but lifelong and exemplary punishment.

Public disbelief to a certain extent in Stagg's guilt led prejudice to transfer the suspicion of guilt to Trooper Lomas, who apprehended him. Police officials admitted some years later, that Lomas had been suspected from the very earliest stages of the case, of being a member of the cattle stealing gang in which Stagg and Gofton were both involved. While any individual member of Gofton's gang of course could be said to have had a motive for getting him out of the way, and might have adopted the mode attributed to Stagg, I would not have alluded to this topic had Mr Lomas himself not recently brought the matter before the South Australian public. Several years after the execution of Stagg, Sir Charles Cooper received a communication from England that a man named Lomas, while in a state of lunacy and believing himself to be at the point of death, had confessed that he murdered Gofton. On receipt of this intelligence the Judge, who was a most amiable and conscientious man, became mentally distressed. He communicated with the police authorities, and with some of them visited the scene of the murder, and, I am assured on good authority, became convinced that the murder was committed by Lomas.

As recently as 1874 the Trooper Lomas presented himself at the office of the *Register* newspaper in Adelaide, and in reference to Gofton's murder stated that he remained in the colony ten years after the execution of Stagg. He then proceeded to England, leaving his wife and three daughters here. In England he was surprised to read an extract from a colonial journal, wherein was contained an account of his lunacy and confession, both statements being false. From England he voyaged to Western Australia in 1857, where he had remained ever since and had acquired considerable property. He stated that two persons here could prove that he [Lomas] 'was never out of their sight at around the time that Goften was shot'. He said that his reason for visiting Adelaide at this late stage was that the authorities of Western Australia made his continuance in their service conditional on his clearing his character from suspicion in relation to the Goften affair. Well might the Editor of the *Register* be justified in titling this narrative 'A strange story'; but its strangest part is the concluding paragraph, which reads thus: 'He alleges that after the murder and at the *post-mortem* examination when the body was exhumed, he took from the wound in the victim's head a piece of paper which fitted into another piece that had been found in Stagg's possession.'

Whether or not Lomas' confession or his later denial could be believed, or whether they constituted nothing more than

EPISODE VIII

'A strange story' was heatedly debated throughout the colony, and there were many arguments *pro* and *con*, in connection with the tragedy. Let us consider a few of them. Stagg, although admitting atrocities even greater, denied to the last moment of his life having committed that particular act. Much importance was attached to Stagg having carried a gun on the occasion. At that period almost every immigrant from Europe brought a gun with him; and I had at one time nearer seventy than sixty guns, varying in quality from 'Brown Bess' to the most stylish 'Joe Manton', which could not find purchasers. Under such circumstances everybody proceeding into a rural district carried a gun for the purpose of bagging wild turkeys, bronze-wing pigeons, or other game. It was suggested that Stagg, who was Gofton's best friend, and had screened him from justice, could have no motive to kill him. Was not every member of the gang of cattle stealers interested in silencing a man who could not be gotten away from the colony, and whose evidence, if captured, might incriminate the whole of them? Plunder, some said, could not be the motive, because £13.10s was found with the body. Others argued that as the extensive gang with which Gofton was connected had been carrying on a lucrative trade for two or three years, he no doubt had sufficient gold to pay for his passage somewhere, if he could have got on board a craft, and to maintain him afterwards. The few coins found might have been overlooked or left by accident, or for the sake of appearances.

 Why had the body been moved and the coat turned inside out? It is also a strange circumstance that Mr Lomas, having had constant opportunities for doing so, did not deny the slanderous allegation concerning his involvement until thirty-four years after it was first made, and then only because a lucrative position was in jeopardy. In summing up I would like to refer to the statement that a bit of newspaper that had obviously been used as a wad, was extracted from the path of the bullet through

Gofton's head after exhumation. That it should be left there at all is quite amazing. That after remaining for days amid the decomposing brain of a dead man it should be extracted in a condition to fit into the paper from which it was torn is still more amazing. Newspapers then were not printed on vellum nor on cardboard, but as they are now [1878] on paper of a somewhat spongy quality. Other curious circumstances connected with the tragical event might also be argued; but there could be no advantage achieved in doing so at this late stage.

In his written work on South Australia, Mr Anthony Forster remarked that the romance of the colony had yet to be written. The foregoing narrative perhaps might afford an eligible little bit by way of commencement.

episode

IX

South Australian Register 13 March 1878

THE
UNEXPLORED BUSH

This is a much more rare article in Australia than it was thirty or forty years ago. Since that period extensive explorations have been effected in many directions; nevertheless, I have had the gratification several times of journeying in the real bush, by which of course, I do not mean the rural neighbourhoods of towns and sheep stations which I described in a previous episode as 'Glimpses'; on the contrary, by the word 'bush' I intend to designate the wild and untracked wilderness far aloof from even the pioneers of civilisation. The consciousness of being so situated for the first time is a strange and delightful sensation. With your back towards men of your own colour, and your horse's head in the direction of a vast untraversed country, of which little is known beyond its extent, a pleasurable excitement is experienced which was previously unknown. The very vagueness heightens the enjoyment. The nearest approach to it is experienced when an inland-born man first surveys and sails on the open ocean. But launching on the solid wilderness of scrub differs much from commencing a voyage on the liquid wilderness of brine. In a ship you are ever in a crowd, having no power or will of your own, but shut up in a movable cage of which the master-mariner alone has control and guidance. You may have a vast area of water to traverse; but you know that it is water, and you also know exactly to what part the winds are wafting or the hissing steam is driving you. The surface of the ocean may be at one time gently undulating at another convulsed by surging, rushing waves; you may one day be progressing slowly, on another rapidly; but you are nevertheless floating on the same monotonous surface, and the most exciting incident you anticipate is the appearance of another community of voyagers within the circumference of your vision. But in the interior of this irregular country every mile of progress is the penetration of a mystery. The breezes that meet you as they sigh amid the apparently interminable forest seem whispering secrets of the enigmatical regions beyond. The path which probably your horse chooses, his rider only deciding the direction, is perpetually presenting something interesting, because new to you. There are so many unfamiliar flowers beneath your horse's hoofs; so many strange yet simple and melodious notes hailing you from branches and shrubs which border your course; such clouds of black cockatoos, then of white cockatoos; such screaming of numberless parrots – rose-breasted, gold-coloured, green, blue, grey and fifty other colours; such frequent starting of kangaroos, emus, wallabies, wild turkeys, variegated snakes, and lizards, and all sorts of animated things besides, that the mind is constantly fed, yet excited to further craving by the novel and the wonderful. Besides, why should you not see a bunyip or some other enigmatical production of nature?

The platypus, a quadrupedal water-fowl which leaves all the other 'quacks' of the country far behind him, you probably will see, and break your damper and enjoy your tea beside one of his villages. No doubt there are scores of undescribed animals in the enormous continuity of the unknown on which you have entered, and inanimate creations scarcely less interesting. What if you should come in contact with an inland shoal of four-footed air respiring fishes, or a grove of walking trees? Not at all improbable! Such discoveries would be simply Australian. With what varieties of the lords of creation may you fall in? Why should you not, like Peter Wilkins, stumble on people with wings, or rediscover the 'anthropophagi', whose heads Shakespeare describes as growing beneath their shoulders? In any case you will from time to time be brought into contact with tribes of human beings, children of the desert, tough as indiarubber and elastic as whalebone, whose natural covering is a jet black skin, apparently put on them merely because yours is white – or used to be.

I am going to commit an act of great recklessness – that is, to extract from an unpublished poem, the story and scenery that are exclusively Australian, a description of the remote and primitive bush, written amid the objects which it describes. In whatever other particulars the verses may be wanting, they certainly possess the merit of descriptive fidelity:

> The depths of those green solitudes are fraught
> With sweet repose and themes for earnest thought,
> Where he who muses feels himself a part
> Of nature, all uninfluenced by art.
> Flowers spring, expand, fulfil their being's aim,
> Then mingle with the soil from whence they came.
> Life, in all forms, rejoices in its breath,
> And, that recalled, resigns itself to death;
> And thus it should be, evening follows morn;
> To die is natural as to be born!
> No dreary death-bell chills the shuddering air,
> For not a trace of pompous man is there.
> Snakes flash their tinted diamonds in the sun;
> Tall emus stride, the graceful lizards run;
> Butterflies wanton in the genial air;
> Ants throng the ground and birds chirp everywhere.

Odours of leaves with every breeze are blown;
Rank grass shoots up — each shrub-like tuft alone;
Herbs greet the eye with every shade of green;
And flowers of every form glance out between,
Here humbly trailing, climbing there in pride,
Support exacting from the dearth they hide;
On every side, with petals widely spread,
The garnish mallow flaunts its varied red;
Here dance in music many-coloured bells,
Swung as the rustling breeze subsides or swells,
In orderly confusion, great and small
Unfold the instinct which directeth all;
Shrubs of each leaf, and every varying size,
Where nature cast their germs obedient rise;
Each evergreen, unerring finds the place,
Allotted to its own peculiar race,
And quaffs the juices of the fostering soil,
Makes dew, and air, and light its pleasant spoil,
Until, responsive to the season's power,
Its happy essence gushes into flower!

What splendid castles in the air the mind of a traveller in the bush constructs, whether of the fervid sunbeams overhead, of the silver rays of the shadowless moon, or of the scarcely less brilliant ones of large, globular, glistening stars. Most of my colonial castles have been built at night. My sweetest waking dreams have been enjoyed when those of slumber would have been more seasonable. Never have I more forcibly experienced reflective mental pleasure than in the depths of an Australian wilderness, when, having with due relish, discussed damper, wild fowl, and tea, I lay beside the flashing and crackling fire, which notwithstanding its size and vivacity, failed to render the enveloping blanket superfluous. It is then that an indescribable sound reaches the ear from indefinite distance; a sound that is distinctly audible, yet most resembles silence – a deep, vague, mysterious moan, which suggest the idea that the enormous wilderness is breathing heavily in slumber. At such moments visions of the future condition of the locality throng into the inviting brain. Down go gum-trees, she-oaks, wattles, and grass-trees; away scamper emus, kangaroos, and turkeys; up spring sheep pastures, cattle runs, farms, gardens, orchards, and vineyards. A little later up rise cities, towns, villages, churches, schools, mechanics' institutes, gas manufactories, waterworks, steam mills, post offices, railways, electric telegraphs, and talking shops *a la* North Terrace. In short all that the unslumbering dreamer beholds with his physical optics is suddenly superseded in imagination by the attributes of a civilised community. Shaking from him his reverie he reflects that what he had merely visioned in anticipation will probably if he be a young man become a palpable reality before the snow of age has descended on his head.

There are men resident on this planet who could travel 'from Dan to Beersheba', and as the result of their journey declare that all in that neighbourhood is barren. There also have been men who resided a dozen or score of years in South Australia, during which time they have converted soap, candles, ironmongery, drapery, treacle, chicory and such like articles into mining shares, sheep runs, freehold lands, town buildings, bank balances, or one or the other of fifty equally good things. All honour to them when they have done so by the exercise of perseverance and integrity. Yet they have returned to Europe knowing no more of the colony generally than they did of Central Africa or the soundings of the alleged open sea at the North Pole. They may have travelled northward as far as Kapunda or the Burra, or southward as far as the Horseshoe, [Noarlunga] Willunga, or even the Goolwa. They have most likely ascended the hills at the back of Adelaide as far as Mount Barker, and are well acquainted with the country extending between Adelaide and the coast from Marino to Port Adelaide. But of the physical characteristics of the country generally or of its political requirements they know nothing. As such men have generally been looked up to at home as South Australian oracles, the ignorance of people there respecting us cannot be cause of wonder.

Much of the mystery appertaining to our island-continent has of late years been dispelled. The waking-dream which I described in an earlier portion of this article has in many localities become a visible reality. He who thirty-eight or even thirty-five years ago wandered over the colonial wilderness must be astonished now, in whatever direction he travels, to observe the advances which settlement and cultivation have made. While doing so, he is apt to compare the amount of work done with our comparatively small population, and thence to honour us with credit for industry and perseverance, only part of which is due to us. Much of the transformation which he beholds was effected by muscular arms which are no longer counted in our census – by able and industrious men, some of whom are in their graves, while many more have transferred their capital of money and labour to other lands.

The four preliminary sections intervening between Adelaide and Kensington, and which were the site of the now flourishing suburb of Norwood, afforded a beautiful specimen of primitive country. The magnitude and symmetry of the trees, the sparkling clearness of the running water, the multitude of wild flowers beneath and of birds above combined to produce this result. Just after the sale of these sections in blocks of two and a half acres had been announced, I chanced to ride through them from the hills to Adelaide with one of our principal colonists. He remarked that it was a pity to deface so much beauty with dusty roads and bricks and mortar. I suggested that one kind of beauty would be superseded by another - that in place of what we were then admiring would spring up villas and cottages surrounded by cultivated flowers, fruit trees, and vineyards. He admitted the probability, and it has been fully realised. Similar transitions are extending over hundreds of miles, and probably will hereafter extend continuously from Port Adelaide to Port Darwin. How will Australia rank among the nations then? I hope, nevertheless, that to a very remote period some characteristic portions of bush country will retain their primitive condition, in order that our descendants may become acquainted with features of the land as found by their forefathers on arrival from thickly populated Europe.

episode

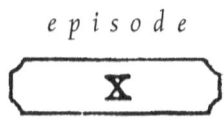

South Australian Register 27 March 1878

WATER AND THE WANT OF IT

In a new country, the only thing more important than obtaining wholesome food is the necessity of obtaining supplies of pure, fresh water. I must devote a whole chapter to the history of our much abused River Torrens, and therefore need only to remark here that household supplies of the indispensable fluid were brought to our houses and tents from the river in carts, except in the few incidents where wells had been sunk at great expense and with greatly varied results.

Nothing in Adelaide proved more whimsical than underground water at that time. A well could sometimes be sunk to a level that produced drinkable water; yet often, by extending the depth of the well by just a few feet the liquid became salt or brackish.

Throughout the city, and the colony in general, salt water and fresh water could be found at alternating depths, quite often very close together. I once travelled with a party in the extreme western portion of this colony along a gully extending several miles. A series of waterholes were situated in this gully. Some were fresh, while an equal number, sometimes as close as several feet apart, were salt.

EPISODE X

Many were the lives lost in various parts of the colony in those days chiefly from want of water while travelling the bush, and many were the hairbreadth escapes from that horrible form of death. Those who have been without water in a hot climate for twenty-four hours will tell you that no other suffering they have ever endured equalled the intense anguish, both mental and physical, which attended protracted thirst.

The country between Adelaide and Encounter Bay was particularly liable to such casualties. In 1838 the police captured a man named Morgan, a companion of the recently executed Michael Magee, at Encounter Bay, and attempted to convey him to Adelaide for trial. A large portion of the territory between the two places was a desert of scrub and sand, thickly interspersed with boulders of stone. The practice of the police at the time when conveying a prisoner was to fasten him to a tree at every halt. During their journey with Morgan they several times lost their way and regained it with difficulty. The weather was excessively hot, locations of fresh water springs were unknown, and the supply of water with which they had started was nearly exhausted. The food also had nearly all been consumed. Under these circumstances, Morgan, who showed advanced symptoms of exhaustion - a condition which was exaggerated by the restrictions imposed by the handcuffs he was forced to wear - laid himself down on the ground and refused to move another step onward. Neither threats of being shot by the policemen, or of being left there to die of thirst could encourage the prisoner to move.

The constables were almost exhausted too, and perhaps were as much encumbered by their weapons as the prisoner was by his manacles. Death from starvation, heat, and thirst was staring them in the face, so they made Morgan fast to a tree in a secluded spot by passing his arms around it and securing his wrists with handcuffs. The policemen then pushed on for Adelaide without him. For four days the prisoner remained in this predicament, his frantic struggles to free himself from his shackles only succeeded in having them cut deeper into the flesh of his wrists. He was exposed to the scorching heat during the day, piercing chills at night, and suffering privation both of water and food. Ravenous birds screamed around him during daylight and wild dogs prowled near him at night, venturing every hour closer and closer to him, waiting for exhaustion to overcome him. By day, flies perched upon his raw wrists, and when they retired at sunset, mosquitoes continued the assault. After four days he was found alive by a police party who had been dispatched to search for him. When discovered, he was covered by thousands of bush flies that had settled on him, some of them having deposited their hideous living spawn upon his face and hands. A few hours more would have terminated the career of the untried felon by a death too horrible to contemplate.

Morgan was successfully conveyed to Adelaide where, on 19 April, 1838 he was sentenced to life imprisonment in the penal settlements of Van Diemen's Land.

A few months later another remarkable escape from death occurred in the same neighbourhood. A murder had been or was supposed to have been committed by one of the whalers at Encounter Bay. Mr Nicholls, then Coroner, started from Adelaide on horseback for the purpose of holding an inquest at the whale fishery there. Beyond Willunga he lost his way and then his horse. Eight days later he made his appearance at the Police Station at Encounter Bay crawling on his hands and knees. Great indeed was his exhaustion, for during the long period he had tasted no ordinary food nor drunk water; the little sustenance he obtained consisted of roots and other vegetable substances and he somewhat alleviated his thirst by chewing tendrils of the she-oak. The poor fellow's boots adhered so tightly to his feet that it was necessary to cut them away piecemeal and with great care. The last time I talked with Mr Nicholls we discussed his past deeds and fearing that my memory might mislead me as to the duration of his lonely misadventure in the wilderness, I enquired of him as to the fact, and the term of eight days was made apparent by reference to dates.

Immediately after Mr Nicholls' notable incident I had occasion to visit Encounter Bay, and I made more minute enquiries in regard to the route than I might otherwise have done. Major O'Halloran, who was then Commissioner of Police, kindly furnished me with full directions for my journey, and with letters to officers in charge at the police tents at Willunga and Encounter Bay requesting that accommodation be offered to me wherever it was within their power to do so. The Major especially cautioned me regarding the distant water of Lake Victoria, which would become visible to me a few miles beyond Willunga and which I might mistake for the shores of Encounter Bay.

Soon after daybreak next morning I presented myself at Chambers' stables to be introduced to my four-legged travelling companion. Mr Chambers' assistant brought forth a powerful-looking animal, well suited for the journey, but with legs so long and back so high in the air that I almost felt the need of a ladder to mount the beast I succeeded, however, in reaching the top without one. 'Does he know the Southern Districts?' I enquired. 'Oh, yes,' replied the stable hand,'he took Mr Nicholls down south two or three weeks ago.' At these words I felt an uncomfortable sensation beneath my waistcoat, and if the distance to the ground had not been so great I think I should have got down again immediately. The information, however, was useful to me.

About three miles beyond Willunga I saw the blue lake,

and the mountainous horse beneath me showed great determination to travel in that direction, caring little whether he took me along or parted company with me on the road, as he had done with Mr Nicholls. The determination of the horse to reach the lake was later explained to me. Very simply, the horse had spent several months of his infancy at the lake, the sight of which rekindled fond memories of other days and a desire to renew old friendships.

In spite of his protests to the contrary, I succeeded eventually in guiding his four excessively long legs to Encounter Bay. I spent a very pleasant night at Encounter Bay in bush fashion in the police tent. Captain Hart came ashore from his vessel, which was moored in the harbour, and offered to take me on board and show me about. Having very little time at my disposal I had to reluctantly decline his hospitality. That night I was treated to a delicious feast of freshly cooked crayfish which had been brought to the police camp by some of the local natives; and as these most sought-after crustaceans were then rarely procurable in Adelaide, I was desirous of taking a couple back with me. Accordingly, I agreed with a native to supply me with two as soon after sunrise next morning as possible for a specific sum. I arose at sunrise, and on looking from the tent saw a spear driven into the ground opposite the entrance, by which sign I knew that the enterprising aborigine was engaged in fulfilling his contract. I could however, not await his arrival with the delicacy, but of course left the amount which we had agreed upon with the police, to compensate him for his effort.

Although my horse did not succeed in getting to his favourite feeding-ground, he succeeded in losing me on the journey back. At noon I became convinced that I was proceeding on the wrong track in that horrible desert of sand, stumps, and granite blocks. There was a blazing sun above me,

EPISODE X

and my water-bottle had been empty three hours; all vegetation around me was scorched to the point where it seemed ready to ignite. These things together with the thought of subsisting for a week or two on berries, roots, and she-oak tendrils, were by no means appealing to me. I had just made up my mind to let the stalking monster carry me to Lake Victoria or anywhere else when I saw something white among the bushes. This welcome apparition proved to be a friend who was in charge of a party of surveyors who were mapping out the future road. He pointed the way to his tent, where he said I should find pure, cold water. On seeing how hot I was he decided to join me, and from a small cupboard within the tent produced a bottle of that amber fluid that only the natives of Scotland seem capable of producing successfully. To each of two tumblers he adding a small measure of the fluid, he then added a larger quantity of water. No drink I have ever had, either prior to that time or since, has ever tasted better. Expressing my most sincere gratitude I took leave of his most welcome company and following his directions continued on my amended, homeward course. I reached Adelaide soon after nightfall and very gratefully descended from my mountainous beast of burden without spraining either of my ankles.

Not long after the date of the foregoing occurrence, Major O'Halloran paid for a well to be sunk as a convenience to passing travellers. It was positioned on the roadside not far from his residence, on the hill which bears his name. As some people still passed without discovering the well, a board was placed in a conspicuous position bearing the inscription in large letters, 'O'Halloran's Well'. I am sorry to say that shortly after the sign was installed an ungrateful vandal, who had taken advantage of the Major's benevolence to refresh himself and his horse, had the impertinence to deface the lower part of the board with bold chalked letters, which defied obliteration by the showers of the ensuing winter. Beneath the words 'O'Halloran's Well' the vandal had audaciously inscribed 'Very glad to hear it! Hope Mrs O'Halloran is well also!'

episode

XI

South Australian Register 3 April 1878

POSTAL COMMUNICATION

Immigrants to Australia at the present time cannot even begin to imagine the sense of isolation which was felt by pioneers on arrival here thirty-eight or forty years ago, completely deprived of European news and family matters. In those days of sailing vessels, from three to six months were occupied in the voyage to Australia and any tidings of the world we left behind would require at least that amount of time between dispatch and arrival. Twelve months was consequently the average period calculated to elapse between written communication with Europe and receipt of letters in reply. Consequently it was not unusual for the great delay in anxiously awaited news of a sick or aged friend or relative to worry the settler's mind for months.

Perhaps no invention of social significance has made itself more obvious during the last three-quarters of a century than the overseas telegraph. It has single-handedly been responsible for the virtual annihilation of distance, and has facilitated intercourse between widely separated nations and individuals.

Post Office arrangements in England, even fifty or sixty years ago were sad, bungling affairs. Relatives in rural districts residing comparatively only a few miles apart seldom heard of each other perhaps during an interval of years.

At that time very few of the English peasantry could write,

and it was a very extraordinary occasion that could induce them to employ a scribe. Even when letters were sent, slow carts and lazy boys on horseback, not to mention boggy roads and occasional floods, rendered the news somewhat antiquated. Also the frequent petty vexations which occurred in relation to postage, which was sometimes paid by the sender of the letter, sometimes by its recipient, if found, were very inconvenient. When subsequently public attention was earnestly given to teaching the masses to read and to write, the necessity for adopting some system for the exchange of letters became imperative, and necessity in that case, as in others, became the mother of invention.

That much inconvenience should have been felt in the early days of this colony in regard to communication with 'home' was inevitable. How that word 'home' clings to us old folk even now! When our immediate descendants use the word it will indicate the country to which we have brought them, or in which they have been born; and thus it should be. Sometimes the non-arrival of letters, at others their long delay on the way, were subjects for complaint in Adelaide. On the other hand people at home who wanted all possible information about the new and paradoxical territory complained that their friends here were not sufficiently prompt in their communications.

Apart from South Australia or Australia at large, complaints of the forgetfulness or negligence of emigrating connections are probably as antiquated as the invention of ships – certainly as ancient as the art of writing. That the charge is true, as regards most men who expatriate themselves to distant and savage countries, cannot be denied. They promptly communicate the fact of their arrival, add a few letters at lengthening intervals and then subside into silence. However inexcusable this conduct may be it is by no means unaccountable. Lord Byron wrote with a lamentable absence of charitable feeling:

*Well really if a man won't let us know
That he's alive, he's dead or should be so!*

The charge, however, applies, although perhaps in a minor degree, to correspondents left in the old country. In many instances it is the departed relative or friend who realises the adage 'out of sight, out of mind'. Charles Lamb admits, and in some degree accounts and offers excuse for this home remissness in a letter characteristically rambling and bantering which he addressed a very long while ago, to a friend who had emigrated to New South Wales. He commences thus:

> *My dear F—— When I think how welcome the sight of a letter from the world where you were born must be to you in that strange one to which you have been transplanted, I feel some uneasiness regarding my long silence. But, indeed, it is no easy effort to set about a correspondence at our distance. The weary world of waters between us oppresses the imagination. It is difficult to conceive how a scrawl of mine should ever stretch across it. It is a sort of presumption to expect that one's thoughts should live so far. It is like writing for posterity.*

This effect of distance between writer and reader, or rather lapse of time between the writing and reading a communication, Lamb illustrates thus:

> *What security can I have that what I now send you for truth shall not, before you get it, unaccountably turn into a lie? For instance, our mutual friend 'P' is at this present writing – my now – in good health and enjoys a fair share of worldly reputation. You are glad to hear it. This is natural and friendly, but at this present reading – your now – he may possibly be in the Bench or going to be hanged.*

While copying the foregoing I was reminded that the last time I was in company with Mr Lamb the topic 'Australia' turned up. Neither South Australia nor Victoria was then thought of. I expressed a willingness to emigrate to the great south land, and the amiable essayist denounced the admission with affected severity. He said when a man, born amid literature and advancing art and science, desired to cross the world to live with kangaroos, he evinced 'a barbarous inclination'. He kindly added, with a significant glance at me, that no doubt the meaty ones would die in character and be buried in the stomachs of blackfellows.

Lamb's playful argument, which applied with full force to this colony when it was first peopled, has now been rendered obsolete. Circular steaming and electric telegraphs have brought the conflicting *nows* into much closer proximity. Nevertheless, the tardy colonial letter-writer is entitled to much more allowance than his correspondent on the other side of the globe. The latter remains in his habitual sphere of action; the former has entered a newly organised community and is surrounded by unfamiliar circumstances. If head or hands are his only capital, and especially if a family is dependent on him, while his future is problematical, his present will demand all the efforts of both. Perhaps he writes one or two hopeful letters and, his hopes not being immediately realised, desists. His correspondent does the same until he finds the chasm of non-communication has grown so wide that he shrinks from attempting to leap it, and the longer he hesitates the more forbidding does the yawning abyss become. Thus terminate many correspondences, but their termination is rarely if ever attributable to indifference about the country of the colonist's birth. The following verses, written four years after the writer's departure from England, may illustrate the fact. They were composed amid uninfringed bush, between three and four hundred miles from Adelaide, at the seaside, and within seeing distance of a number of small islands with beaches smooth as velvet and white as snow. The writer was alone and the lines, which are embodiments of real feelings operating at the moment, were pencilled in the rough by moonlight.

Homeward Yearnings

The gale of yesterday has died;
The brawling winds as death are still:
In glassy sleep the waves subside,
Outworn by their own stormy will;
Mute is each vale and tree-clad hill,
Save where the wild dog tracks the dew
Or, like the voice of sorrow, shrill,
And sadly plains the lorn curlew.

Twilight – day's ghost – scarce seen, is gone
And ocean rolls in light afar,
Swathing, each in its silvery zone,
Yon isles, which her loved infants are
Far in heaven's depth gleams many a star –
Ah! Not the stars my boyhood knew –
And mounting o'er the horizon's bar
The moon makes pale the cloudless blue.

What saw'st thou, Moon, short hours ago,
In my far native hemisphere?
Did kindred eyes gaze from below,
And lips sigh – 'Would that he were here?'
Say, didst thou gild that turret sere,
'Neath which an old man worn with thought
Led my first prayers, and made more dear
To all the sacred lore he taught?

Did thy beams clasp that rustic home
Round which a pensive dreaming boy
With Shakespeare's magic page I'd roam,
Or snatch from Byron sterner joy?
Where Spenser's rhyme gave sweet employ,
Beside the trout-stream in the vale,
Do the old elm trees still decoy
The pensive, thence thy rise to hail?

What saw'st thou, Moon! My boyhood's friend!
Companion! 'Neath yon distant sky?
Do forms beloved in old scenes blend?
Does laughter flash from cheek and eye
When Christmas mirth is mantling high?
Does still the merry viol sound,
And feet as merrily reply
Amid the dance's varied round?

Yet say, what saw'st thou? Eyes grown dim,
Though not with age? And faces pale,
Yet not from pain? And sturdy limb
Grown feeble from some unknown ail?
O'er what new grave do mourners wail?
Who still endure the ills of life,
With strength unbowed or tremors frail?
And who have fled life's feverish strife?

One moment could I doff this clay
And spring forth an unbodied mind,
I would outspeed light's swiftest ray,
And, leaving thy gross beams behind,
Reach scenes by memory enshrined!
Shunning the footprints of decay,
I'd pause where I might objects find
Whose old forms have not passed away!

EPISODE XI

Fond wish, yet not more fond than vain!
Here, where the savage hath his home,
My soul endures the rambling chain,
And scarce on fancy's wings may roam.
What am I? bubble of the foam,
Cast on this shore by life's rough sea;
An hour to quiver 'neath heaven's dome,
And then, unnoted, cease to be.

In the earlier days of this colony the interest taken in the comparatively rare arrival of vessels from Europe was intense. The exclamation, 'A ship in sight', acted with the force of electricity, and was propelled from tent to cottage until the whole Lilliputian community had become aware of the fact. People got up in the middle of the night – however cold, dark, and dirty it might be – walked to the Post Office notwithstanding the unreasonableness of the hour, and waited until the mailbags were received. That important public establishment was a weatherboard cabin of two rooms at the north-eastern corner of King William Street.[1] The business was afterwards removed to somewhat more commodious apartments at the north-western corner of the same street.[2] Then succeeded an unambitious predecessor to our present noble building. In all three localities for several years Captain Watts was the presiding official, one military brother having succeeded another in the office; and each did his best to alleviate inevitable vexations by uniform courtesy, and by making allowance for unavoidable circumstances.

A generation or two back great were the impediments to communication between relatives and other connections even in Europe; and as a matter of course additions to those inconvenience accrued in distant and isolated communities. In the year 1840 I forwarded a letter to London wherein I incautiously enclosed a small lock of hair appertaining to the first Australian born member of my family. There was an understanding between my relatives and myself that we would mutually post our letters postage unpaid, as we were afflicted by the notion that they were more certain to arrive if payment was conditional on delivery. That letter cost in England between four and five shillings, much to my vexation, although I knew that the money was most cheerfully paid. Had the system of uniform pre-payment with official certificate thereof endorsed then prevailed I should have been spared that and many similar annoyances, as would thousands of other individuals.

These colonies, in common with the nation at large, are greatly indebted to Sir Rowland Hill, who has lived to see the results and reap the reward of his labours in the cause of Post Office reform. It has, however, occurred to me that he is credited wholly or chiefly with the less important feature of his achievement. The establishment of cheap and uniform postage throughout the United Kingdom was a social and financial improvement, yet it was one which might have suggested itself to Joseph Hume of 'sum-total-of-the-whole' celebrity; but the idea of revolutionising the entire system by substituting for payment with money, whether when posting or on delivery, compulsory use of previously purchased and officially authenticated stamps, evinced something Newtonian by its simplicity and effectiveness; it at once relieved the Post Office of rough, unpleasant and responsible work, and conferred incalculable benefit on the whole community.

episode

XII

South Australian Register 17 April 1878

OLD COLONIAL WEATHER

There can be no doubt that the occupation by civilised man of an ancient and extensive desert modifies the climate of the locality and renders it better adapted for the requirements of his race. I think the settled districts of South Australia afford unequivocal evidence of this fact. Among the visible agencies producing these results, two of the more obvious and effective, although not perhaps acting in unison, are the clearing away of timber and cultivation of the soil. Those who in the early days of the colony saw storms of rain descending with almost tropical violence on the smooth and hard-baked plains of Adelaide and instantly running off as from a metallic surface, flooding in their way gutters, creeks, and rivers, can fully assess the contrast presented at the present time. Now hundreds of miles north, south, and east of Adelaide have been penetrated by the plough or spade, and consequently temporarily detain the rain, part of which subsequently filtrates to the nearest water course, while the remainder is either absorbed by vegetation or evaporates into the atmosphere.

These and other processes consequent on our settling here have, as old colonists agree, considerably modified our weather. My present business, however, is with that and kindred phenomena as we found them on arrival in the colony. That the climate is not of a deadly nature I personally furnish an instance.

I have resided almost constantly for more than thirty-eight years in South Australia. My occupations have been chiefly carried on in the open air, and the noontide hours have always been included in my working period, yet never was I detained from business by weather of any kind, except on one remarkable day, to which I will presently allude more particularly. I have been for weeks and sometimes for months in the remote bush, and have then, through wet weather and dry, slept frequently under a tarpaulin, a blanket, wallaby skins, and sometimes the open sky, my couch on such occasions having generally been the grass covered earth or the wave-levelled sand of the sea beach, yet I never sustained a deterioration to my health as a consequence.

Undoubtedly our midday summer heat is occasionally excessive, and in an occasional season like that last, the first of its kind which I have experienced, aided by increased exhalations, rendered the atmosphere oppressive and for a time unwholesome. In the early days of Adelaide the intense heat of solar rays reflected from a bare dry surface was trying to European constitutions, but only produced momentary inconvenience and was rarely the occasion of injury. Instances of *coup-de-soleil* were, as they now are, less frequent than might have been anticipated, and were in most cases attributable to carelessness. Yet most of the business arrangements which occasioned the congregating of numbers took place at or about noon. It was often suggested that in the summer season a cessation of business for two or three hours in the middle of the day should take place, but the suggestion was never acted on – a clear proof that its necessity has never made itself imperatively felt.

I have said that there was one day on which I absented myself from business by constraint of weather; that was 'Black Thursday', 6th February, 1851, a day without parallel even in this hemisphere. I resided then at the foot of the hills, between three and four miles from Adelaide. My horse was saddled at the usual hour, and I had ridden a few hundred yards from my gate, when the animal recoiled from a blast which resembled the combined and concentrated vapour issuing from a thousand brick kilns. I returned him to the stable, leaving the saddle on, for I thought that tempest would soon relieve the atmosphere of its sulphurous burden; but as the day wore on the sky became denser and darker, the air hotter and more noxious. Feeling certain that, for once, business in Adelaide would be suspended, I liberated the horse from his saddle, left him to luxuriate in a cool stable on new hay and fresh-drawn well water, and kept down my own temperature by frequent and copious sprinkling of rooms and verandah with cold water, and the personal imbibition of cups of hot liquids. That day fruits of all kinds were literally roasted on the trees. Leaves of trees and bushes and the upper portions of vegetables were so thoroughly oxidised by the heat that a mere touch reduced them to powder.

The whole of Australia appears to have been subjected to the inclemency of that unearthly day, and it assumed much greater severity in Victoria and New South Wales than in South Australia. When engaged in gold digging in the adjoining colony in 1852 several Victorian settlers for the time similarly engaged, narrated to me extraordinary scenes which they had witnessed in the uncultivated districts of that colony on Black Thursday. Enormous bush fires were burning in every direction, sheep and cattle were roasted alive, and several human lives were sacrificed. In some instances, while one fire was rushing and roaring along, another conflagration would burst forth a few miles ahead, as if the eager demon of fire had vaulted unseen over the intervening space. It is a curious fact, to which I can personally bear testimony, that the aboriginals of Victoria uniformly attributed the origins of gold to Black Thursday, which immediately preceded its discovery. I have heard many of them insist on the fact with great earnestness. This is almost proof that they were not acquainted with the existence of the precious metal until its discovery by Europeans. Corroboration of this assumption is afforded by the absence of gold from among substances which previously they were accustomed to employ for use or ornament. I used, while working at the gold diggings, to consider the latter a remarkable fact, taking into account the rich colour of the metal and its prevalence at the time of which I write. Of course natives could not be expected to unearth it, or, if they did, to distinguish it from accompanying earth or stone; but when I was there I found spots on the surface where after rain small golden beads glistened in the sunshine sufficiently to attract observation. On such occasions I have in a few hours scraped together with my pocket-knife as many minute nuggets from among the blades of grass as would fill a dessert spoon. These varied in size from the dimensions of sparrow to swan shot. It struck me as strange that none of these pretty little beads were ever used for the personal adornment of lubra or piccaninny.

We used to have extremely cold as well as extremely hot weather in Adelaide, and I am inclined to think that the alternation of extremes was more marked and sudden then than now. Ice in the streets was not an uncommon spectacle. Frozen gutters we witnessed last winter, but the ice was less massive and melted away far more quickly than in previous times.

There was also a slight fall of snow, which from its rarity excited great curiosity. Once, and but once, I witnessed a snowstorm here worthy of England. I think it must have occurred in the winter of 1840, but have no means of referring to the correct date. I was at that time editing a newspaper, which was printed at the northern side of Adelaide, while my residence was at the southern extremity. The sun had not risen when I left the office.

EPISODE XII

A little sleet was falling, by no means an uncommon occurrence, while hailstorms of extreme violence were frequent, and sometimes inflicted much damage on buildings and gardens. In a few minutes the sky grew much darker, and a heavy fall of snow commenced - real feathery snow - in flakes as large as sixpences and shillings floating gradually down and accumulating where they fell. By the time I reached home the ground, trees, roofs of houses, and all other inert objects were clad in a uniform of glistening white. Not a bush nor flower displaying its own colours was visible in my garden, and I cast heavy fleeces from my outer garments as I discarded them. Many a game at snowballs I played next day with boys, some of them older than myself, originators of the colony, whom I will not name for fear of them being ridiculed for indulgence in such a pastime. Snow in large patches remained visible in the township for days, and the Mount Lofty range of hills presented a strange and picturesque appearance. On riding, even three weeks after, in the neighbourhood of Mount Barker, I saw masses of snow of considerable depth still lying in gullies and other sheltered spots, where, no doubt, they had been drifted. That such a fall is of very rare occurrence was proved by the testimony of natives. The young had never beheld such a scene, the middle-aged had heard of, and the most antiquated patriarchs had witnessed something like it.

One of the phenomena that used to startle new arrivals was the whirling dust-column. Multitudinous lines of buildings had not then been erected to curtail the free exercise of their gambols in Adelaide. Some of these columns traversed miles before dissolution, were of extreme height, and possessed of such mechanical force that while spinning along they would catch into their vortex and raise from the ground straw, rags, papers, sticks, and all such 'unconsidered trifles', I once saw moderately sized account books and an empty cash-box thus exalted to a very respectable distance from the ground. One day I was standing in front of our little wooden Courthouse in conversation with Mr Charles Mann, when a tall column went rushing and roaring past us, increasing its bulk at every yard of progress. We estimated its height at a mile. When it had proceeded onward about a quarter of a mile it stopped suddenly, expanded its substance, laterally to about twenty times its travelling breadth, when a new compact column darted up in its centre, and resuming the journey left the discarded atoms behind it, like the cast skin of an enormous serpent. One remarkable characteristic of these dust whirls is that when they have free course for their progress the surrounding atmosphere is breathlessly still. In 1840 I was taken into custody by one on North Terrace, which was a favourite resort of these dusty freaks of nature. I had just descended the steps of the Bank of South Australia, when I found myself in the embrace of a massive pillar travelling with great velocity. It screwed me halfway round, and imparted to me the sensation of being about to ascend into the air, which exaltation, however, I escaped. When released from the hug of my dusty friend, I brushed from my face a considerable quantity of his discarded substance, and beheld near me three ladies of my acquaintance, who were clad in white garments; these had been left unsoiled by the unclean monster which had chosen his path close to them. I regret to add they were heartless enough to laugh loudly at my involuntary 'Jim Crow' action, and at my subsequent resemblance to an obsolete statue in some neglected shrine.

Another phenomenon that I often observed, and which occurred only when the atmosphere was motionless, was the sudden snapping and falling of trees apparently sound, and some of them of gigantic size. The crash which ensued amid surrounding silence was peculiarly emphatic. Occasionally this apparently unnatural stillness was suddenly broken by a sort of hot, dry wind not unlike the dreaded Sirocco of North Africa. It vented its fury for a few minutes and then left all around motionless and silent as before, but not, when forcing its way through woodlands, until it had torn off sturdy branches, and even uprooted massive trees. One afternoon, on my return from Adelaide towards my then residence at the foot of the Mount Lofty range of hills, I had nearly passed through the forest, which is now called Norwood, when behind me I heard a din composed of roaring, hissing, cracking, and other contending sounds. The wind-fiend was half a mile to rearward but approaching direct towards me. The atmosphere was perfectly calm and oppressively heavy. All trees near me seemed asleep; not a leaf was moving. The advancing atmospheric wave made itself terribly apparent by flying branches, tall trees swayed and bent like twigs, and an attendant cloud of sticks, bark, leaves and dust. I put my mare to her speed for a few seconds, but finding flight fruitless I dismounted and chose as standing-ground the clearest spot close at hand, by which time the progressive but momentary chaos had reached me. My steed snapped her bridle and galloped off. I lost my hat, endured a few smart cuts from small substances driven with violence against me, and then all was calm and peaceful as before. The remainder of my journey home was in the wake of the aerial demon, which had done no mischief beyond impairing the symmetry of several gum trees, but, on the other hand, had ingratiated himself with the thrifty housewives by providing an abundance of firewood without the intervention of axe or saw. At my own door lay an enormous and sound branch of a gum tree which had the appearance of having been twisted off.

On leaving England I anticipated witnessing tempest in more terrific forms than it assumes here; but although I have seen thunderstorms in all parts of this colony, amid the hills and on the plains, I have never, either recently or in the olden time of the colony, witnessed one to equal in ferocity of some which I beheld in England many years ago. The calm beauties of moonlight and starlight are so often reflected in our transparent Australian sky although occasionally now it seems more obscured by vapour than it formerly was. I used to frequently see lunar rainbows, both single and double, some of them possessing great beauty. I have not witnessed any lately, but perhaps I have just not been looking for them.

Nathaniel Hailes, from a sketch by S.T. Gill

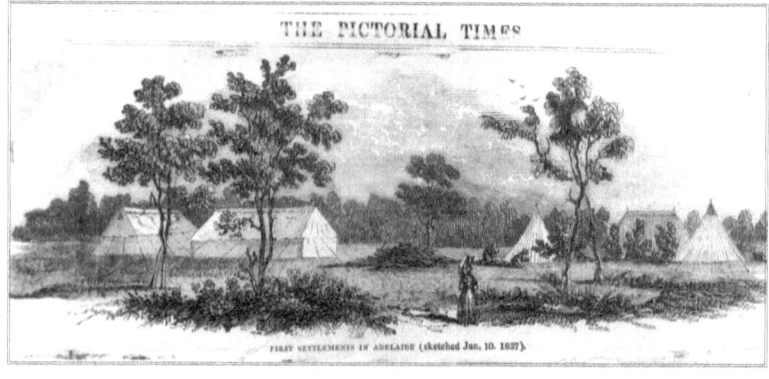

FIRST SETTLEMENTS IN ADELAIDE (sketched Jan. 10, 1837).

TOP: Glenelg, 1839   ADELAIDE CITY ARCHIVES
BOTTOM: Adelaide, the first settlement   ADELAIDE CITY ARCHIVES 1288

Charles Mann, photographic reproduction of a painting
SSL:MLSA:B6620

TOP: Home of T.S. O'Halloran, 1865 SSL:MLSA:B45375
BOTTOM: First Government House, Adelaide 1837 SSL:MLSA:B6705

Osmond Gilles, from a sketch by S.T. Gill
SSL:MLSA:B347

TOP: The German village of Klemzig, 1845 SSL:MLSA:B7188/10
BOTTOM: The execution of Michael Magee from a sketch by J.M. Skipper, 1838 SSL:MLSA:B7797

TOP: The remains of Frank Hawson being prepared for reburial at Kirton Point, 1911   SSL:MLSA:B54013

BOTTOM: Monument being erected at Port Lincoln in memory of Frank Hawson, 1911   SSL:MLSA:B2254

Nathaniel Hailes

COURTESY OF HIS DESCENDANTS

episode

South Australian Register 1 May 1878

COLONIAL PROGRESSION

The small band of immigrants went to work in real earnest, and in 1839 and 1840 we strived to realise Colonel Gawler's hope that we should soon be not a mere settlement but a colony. The paralysing results of official squabbles began to give place to productive energy. The plough and spade, the axe and trowel were busy in all directions. We began to pay more attention to dress, made fireplaces inside our dwellings instead of outside, constructed public offices of brick and stone instead of weatherboards and palings, built houses of two storeys instead of one, and in time learned to carry up a staircase inside instead of connecting the upper window with the ground by means of a ladder outside.

We even made a start in the ship-building line, and commenced our maritime navy by building the OG at Glenelg. The name was chosen in honour of Osmond Gilles and the craft was built for the South Australian Company. Her exact capacity I forget, but I think it did not fall short of eight tons.[3]

The occasion of her launch was indeed a grand affair. A large tent was erected and crowded with invited guests, who were liberally supplied with a champagne luncheon.

Every vehicle in and around Adelaide less heavy than a wagon was in demand, and horses hitherto better acquainted with plough harness than a saddle were promoted to be saddle-horses for the occasion. The morning was bright, balmy, and consequently inviting. The bonnets and dresses and bouquets that were paraded on the Bay-Road that morning would have done no discredit to Greenwich Fair. About noon torrents of rain began to descend without intermission and forgot to leave off for twelve hours. This persistent inclemency of the weather compelled close adherence to the tent and the company's excellent champagne. That and a profusion of bottled beer induced such sunshiny radiance inside that the unceasing patter and splash without enhanced the enjoyment rather than otherwise. But, as Burns tells us:

> *Pleasures are like poppies spread,*
> *We seize the flower, its bloom is shed;*
> *Or like the snowflakes in a river —*
> *A moment white, then lost for ever;*
> *Or like the Borealis race,*
> *That flit ere you can point their place;*
> *Or like the rainbow's lovely form,*
> *Evanishing amid the storm.*

The time to separate at length came, or rather the proper time for proceeding homeward had long passed. Still the sky was one ebon mass, the earth a shallow lake and as for the big, round, cold raindrops, the popular comparisons of 'cats and dogs' gives no adequate idea of them. Eventful were the occurrences of that night as a too bright morning rendered evident. Horses arrived at their stables riderless, and some of their owners reached the same neighbourhood a few hours afterwards. Vehicles were discovered unaccountably stuck in holes, lodged against fallen trees, lying on their sides or backs, or in any other position inconsistent with progress, while their previous occupants and the unhappy quadrupeds which had been associated in the dilemma had slid, waded, or scrambled somewhere or other.

Then Colonel Gawler was a military man, one of Wellington's captains, as his predecessor in the office of Governor, Captain Hindmarsh, was one of Nelson's heroes, and both were men to whom the country for which they fought were deeply indebted. It was natural that the old Waterloo man should wish to found the nucleus of an army, and accordingly early in the year 1840 such an institution was established. Its constitution, if exhibited in detail on the pages of the British Army List, would have aroused some amusement.

The regiment consisted, including cavalry and infantry, for no artillery had yet been attached, of eighteen commissioned officers, two non-commissioned officers, and one private. The officers, whose uniforms were handsome and displayed an abundance of gold lace, did good service at the levee on the ensuing Queen's Birthday, which must have been in 1840. We had then begun to practice the genteel, and even to initiate the ceremonious. Not only were military officers at the levee, but the Sheriff and some other civil officers appeared in Court dresses. The effect produced by cocked hats, inexpressibly tight indispensables, silken scarves, and silver shoe-buckles was striking. The worst of it was, the dress swords, or rapiers, kept getting between the courtiers' feet and placed them in danger of tripping and falling. One incident at this first dress levee amused me much. There was an old man, keeper of a very Lilliputian crockery shop situated at the upper end of Hindley Street, who nevertheless presented himself before the Queen's representative that day. He had on a brown coat, worn much thinner than when first brought into use, no gloves, a pair of grey trousers, which evidently were on very distant terms with a pair of nailed shoes beneath them. The old man was gouty, and while hobbling along to make his bow to Colonel Gawler he presented a strange contrast to the black coats, superlative waistcoats, straw-coloured kids, and other refinements by which he was surrounded. I noted the nods, winks, and other sneering indications which followed him. I knew his previous history. He had been a Commissary in the Peninsular war, and his antiquated loyalty would not permit him to neglect its demonstration on Her Majesty's Birthday, although he could not emulate the seemly garb of his neighbours. Some of the dandies were rather astonished when Colonel Gawler smiled approvingly at him, and said a few kind words as he passed.

The most important item of progress was the formation of a Municipal Corporation in 1840, which was stated at the time to be the first purely representative body elected in the Australian Colonies. Whether the fact is so I have not the means of determining. The election took place on the 30th October. Electioneering platforms and polling booths were erected at the junction of Hindley and King William Streets. Flags and other devices ornamented the novel erections, but no party colours, as parties had not commenced to exist. Nineteen citizens were elected – two by 'quorums', an experiment in electioneering which enabled a given number of electors concentrating their votes solely on one candidate to return him. The other seventeen were returned by the qualified colonists generally, who could vote for the whole or any smaller number. To the credit of the men of that day be it spoken that nearly every one voted, and again to their credit be it said not one of those elected had canvassed his fellow-citizens. The names of the first Municipal Council thus spontaneously elected reflect honour on the electors. A list of those names now lies before me; and of the nineteen individuals, I possess knowledge of the deaths of thirteen. At this election I was second on the poll, having received a very few votes less than the late Sir James Hurtle

Fisher. At the election in the following year I was at the head of the poll by a considerable majority over my next colleague. Perhaps after what I wrote just now I should not have stated this. But I see not why a man should not evince pride at having had influence among his fellow-colonists at that early period when the tender plant was being trained into the pasture which the sturdy stem now exhibits. On appearing collectively in the presence of the Governor, Colonel Gawler made some flattering remarks and addressed us most sensibly as to the especial colonial objects to which our earliest attention should be directed.

At that period there was a writer among us who, under the *nom de plume* of 'Timothy Short'[4] published through the newspapers verses, generally satirical, allusive to passing occurrences. These productions possessed no literary merit, but as they indicated and illustrated many early colonial incidents, forgotten by the few and unknown to the many, collectively they would at this period of our history be interesting, but with a few exceptions they have shared the fate of other waste paper. As I chance to possess one of them, which was published in anticipation of the Municipal Council and subsequent to the establishment of the volunteer force, to which among other topics it refers, I insert it here. To understand some of the lines it is necessary for the reader to bear in mind that Mr Charles Mann, our first Advocate-General, was always writing and speaking about the principles of the colony, and that Mr Osmond Gilles, our first Treasurer, was corporeally of a most rotund formation. It is also necessary to be borne in mind that news had just been received in the colony that Her Majesty had been united in wedlock to Prince Albert. The speaker is supposed to stand on the Adelaide plain with his face towards the Mount Lofty range of hills, which reflects his exclamations, as an 'Adelaide Echo', thus:

Man! Yon green hills — each plain and glade,
Where late alone the savage ran
Thou, on new 'PRINCIPLES', hast made
Thine own, and thou art right, O man!
       Echo — Write, O Mann!

And should the Yankee, Russ, or Frank
Invade our acres rich and warm,
Up brave Brigade! — forth every rank!
Bound to thy country, soldier arm!
       Echo — Sold your arm!

Fair country! — dirty town! each street
How bad the muse can but pronounce ill;
Say, how shall we protect out feet?
August, though unborn, Common Council?
       Echo — Come and Counsel!

Haste into being corporate! — haste!
In paving, lighting, watering, train us;
Amend our ways — refine our taste,
Save us from dust attacks, and drain us!
       Echo — Tax and drain us!

The Alderman! Choose them by weight;
Men heavy as Hyde Park Achilles,
'Let men of weight hold civic state!'
A toast! — and send it round O Gilles!
       Echo — Round O Gilles!

The Mayor! A most important matter!
Wend northward, you shall find one there,
Who were he ruddier, sleeker, fatter,
Say, could we find a more fit Mayor?
       Echo — Morphett, Mayor

The Beadle! Choose the man of awe,
Pompous, florid, fat and grinny —
Pick one whose glance and frown are law
To drunkard, drab and piccaninny!
      Echo — Pick and Ninny!

The drums! The men in brass! The throng!
The gilded coach! The mob's scurrilities!
The feast, both plentiful and long!
The speakers, and their liabilities!
      Echo — Lie abilities!

Oh sight sublime! Oh prospect sweet!
Of corslets, crests, and vizor-masks!
And cits parading Hindley Street,
In order all compact, in casques!
      Echo — Packed in casks.

Quail, London! Dingy, smoky, foggy!
Lest we such Cockney height attain,
That we out-Magog and out-Gog thee,
And what within the present reign.
      Echo — The present rain.

'God save the Queen!' Shout every voice,
Our love, our hope, we thus evince!
On thee, too, partner of her choice,
Rely we not a little Prince?
      Echo — A little Prince!

  The Municipal Council got on very well. If we were not always harmonious we were never ill-tempered, and I do not recollect that we were ever betrayed into personalities. I once produced much merriment at the expense of a brother Councillor. The subject was bathing in the Torrens, from which stream at that time we obtained most of our drinking water. The proposition before the Council was that notice boards should be placed along the margin of the stream forbidding bathing at any hour under heavy penalties. The Councillor I allude to observed that measure would not be wholly remedial, as the natives as well as white people were accustomed to bathe there. I suggested that the objection might be overcome by painting the notices in the aboriginal as well as the English language, a suggestion with which he readily concurred. A loud shout of laughter made him aware of his oversight. The aboriginal race of course knew no written language.

But a political tempest was approaching our shores, and when it exploded among us its effects were terrific and affected all classes of colonists.

episode

XIV

South Australian Register 8 May 1878

THE GENERAL SCATTERING

By the foregoing episode it will be seen that the infant colony was advancing steadily, however slowly, in social organisation. But a torpedo was approaching the little colonial craft. Hitherto Adelaide had been the colony. Many of its residents were acquainted only with the pursuits of town life; and many who had been accustomed to rural pursuits, and came out avowedly to engage in agriculture, were prevented from doing so because of the slow progress, which in turn was the result of the miserable official bickerings which marred the very early expansion of South Australia.

Thus consumption was advancing, unaccompanied by production. All were living on their own means, the means of others, or as recipients of the Government expenditure. Our right-minded, right-hearted, but in this instance over-confident Governor, correctly estimating our exhaustless natural resources, took on himself an amount of responsibility which he thought the Commissioners in England would justify. When the Advocate-General, Mr Charles Mann, earnestly reasoned with him on the large drafts which he was sending home, remarking, 'Your Excellency is taking on yourself great responsibility,' his reply was, 'Mr Mann, I am accustomed to taking responsibility upon myself.'

The 'go-ahead' action of the Waterloo veteran, however, did not accord with the mercantile calculations of the London Commissioners and it must be admitted that the Colonel made himself responsible to a great extent. In one year he drew on the Commissioners to the amount of upwards of £123,000. For a time the drafts were paid; but as they continued to arrive thicker, faster, and heavier, they were later systematically dishonoured. The income of the Colony at that time was £30,000 per annum; its annual expenditure was £150,000 to say nothing of a little debt of £300,000 which had been contracted. The dishonour of Colonel Gawler's drafts was the bursting of the torpedo beneath us. The colony was insolvent. The panic was universal. Nearly all the mercantile firms engaged in business to any great extent wound up their affairs. Credits, debits, contra accounts, balances, and such like were meaningless phrases as related to the then present period, just as dinner time and supper time were mere figures of speech when there was nothing in the house to be eaten. A man might have a thousand or two pounds debited in his ledger to highly respectable parties, or he might owe a hundred or two – it came to exactly the same thing. The apparently absurd dogma broached by the first French revolutionists of 'equality' was absolutely realised then by the people of Adelaide. All were equal, for all were equally moneyless. A general amnesty in matters of indebtedness was proposed; this was decidedly superfluous, for, supposing there were a few individuals who could scrape together silver enough to pay Court fees, who would be so mad as to sue a soap-bubble? Besides, there were no parties really indebted. An old authority assures us that 'he nothing owes who nothing has to pay'. Exactly; and as none of us had anything wherewith to pay, of course we were not in debt. There is nothing like logic to elucidate the truth.

Hopes were entertained by the colonists that Colonel

Gawler would receive absolution and that commercial matters would shake down into their accustomed condition. Vain hope! In May 1841, Captain Grey, who was known here as an explorer of Western Australia, arrived unexpectedly, bearing a commission as Governor of the colony. His mission was obvious. With the brashness of youth we had put on a dress coat, silk waistcoat, kid gloves, and broadcloth pantaloons, which we were unable to pay for, and he was commissioned to slip us into a blue shirt, moleskin trousers, and moccasins – and he did it. He speedily reduced the annual expenditure below £30,000. The squeezing, probing, and crushing which the settlers endured during the process of retrenchment can scarcely be imagined.

Meanwhile great were the property sacrifices made, and painful the individual and social sufferings endured. Shops were generally closed. 'To be sold', 'To be let', were inscriptions placarded in all directions on all sorts of tenements. Some employers became labourers. Many heads of families sallied forth, bag and baggage, chose some fertile spot belonging to somebody, anybody, or nobody, and wrested food from the soil, generally in the form of potatoes, often at the risk of its being claimed by an unknown owner when grown. I knew several individuals who were accustomed to the comforts and even luxuries of life, who after toiling energetically five days and a half each week, walked on the Saturday afternoon five, eight, ten and even fourteen miles to Adelaide for flour, groceries, and other necessaries required for the ensuing week's consumption. Too often they had to return with only half their coveted load, cash and credit failing them for the remaining amount required for the week's provisions. As in this state of existence there is no good without some attendant evil, neither probably is there any evil that does not elicit some good. The disruption occasioned by the exploding torpedo by the very scattering which it occasioned was the means of planting farms, gardens, orchards, and vineyards on every side of Adelaide.

The explosion caused some strange minor incidents, many having an affinity to tragedy, some to comedy. Among the former were attempts to sell off treasured household goods, sometimes choice furniture, family relics, paternal watches, wedding rings, books, gifts of loved ones long departed, and many other such treasures, which were quite often disposed of in older colonies, where their intrinsic value might be realised. Among the more ludicrous results were the frequent attempts by inexperienced settlers at bullock driving, fencing, ploughing, well-sinking, and so forth, and the more ridiculous attempts of the navvies to look rustic and bush-like. Then there were some striking inconsistencies of garb. Old European garments, even good ones, must be worn out with all expedition because there was not money with which to buy working type clothing; so you might meet a man attired in a blue serge shirt, moleskin trousers, and something on his head like a dark-coloured mushroom, evidently recent acquisitions, while his feet were encased in a pair of Bond Street wellingtons, and his waist encircled by a richly ornamented vest, the latter two articles of course having arrived in the colony simultaneously with himself. The fragment of the disruption which hoisted me out of Adelaide propelled me to the westward, and landed me in March 1842, at the then infant settlement of Port Lincoln, the name conferred on it by Flinders in 1802.

Captain Grey very kindly appointed me to the vacant office of Clerk of the Court at Port Lincoln, and I had also the duties to perform of Clerk to the Government Resident. The salary was £100 per annum, which considering that flour was £7 per bag, mutton 7 pence per lb., beef, when procurable, 1 shilling per lb., and all other requisites in proportion, was not extravagant pay, more particularly as there were duties to be

EPISODE XIV

performed and many hardships and dangers to be encountered. I was afterwards appointed Registrar, in virtue of which office I married the Resident and several other settlers, and recorded all births and deaths. Subsequently, I fulfilled the offices of Harbour Master and Postmaster for a time; but as regards salary, these additional appointments were strictly honorary. Never mind, I had a gun, and there was abundance of marsupial game on the land, and thousands of palatable birds in the air and on the trees; there were also many well favoured varieties of fish in Boston Bay and Spencer's Gulf. Metaphorically speaking, I was on a hencoop which drifted to me during the storm, and I clung to it for near four years.

Mr Charles John Driver, who will be pleasantly remembered by many old colonists, was appointed Government Resident at the same time that I received the appointment of Clerk of the Court, and the only cutter then trading between Adelaide and Boston Bay - I think her burden was fifteen tons - was engaged to convey us to the latter destination. Mr Driver's arrival in the colony was attended by a domestic calamity. He came from the East Indies, and it was arranged that his mother, sister, and sister's husband should follow him. They sailed from Calcutta, but the vessel never arrived, nor were the passengers ever heard of.

I went on board the little cutter at Glenelg, and as business connected with his brother-in-law's affairs detained Mr Driver in town for several days, I was resident at and off the village during that time. It was not the Glenelg of today, with railway pier, &c; nor was it the Glenelg at which I had first landed three years before; for then it was mere beach, whereas now a few cottages were sprinkled among or behind the sandhills. The most considerable of them was occupied by Mr Wigley, the Resident Magistrate of Adelaide. That house was always open to me, and besides partaking of Mr Wigley's hospitality I learned from him much that appertained to my novel duties in a Court of Law. Still I was chiefly on board. Although our solitary vessel was anchored in deep water, the latter was so clear that gravel, shells, and seaweed at the bottom of Holdfast Bay were distinctly visible, and I spent many pleasant hours in observing denizens of the aqueous world beneath me. I spent one whole afternoon in watching an innumerable and apparently interminable shoal of mackerel, tier above tier, flitting in one continuous mass beneath the keel of the vessel. I subsequently beheld similar myriads of the same palatable fish in Boston Bay, but I have now not seen one at table for many years. Has the mackerel left our coast?

On the afternoon of which I am writing, which was just prior to our setting sail from Holdfast Bay, hundreds of mackerel were caught with baited hooks. I amused myself by flinging broken biscuit amid the limitless and rapidly gliding mass, and observing the speed and grace with which perhaps half a dozen plump and glistening individuals fell out of the streaky-back ranks to dart at one and the self-same crumb. A newly engaged servant of the Resident stood at my elbow observing the results of my somewhat idle employment. He had just arrived from the Emerald Isle, and was every bit as green as the place of his nativity. He was in ecstasy at the commotion which fragments of biscuits produced among the finny myriads beneath. 'Oh, look at them,' he exclaimed, 'do look at them, how they are *diving up* at the biscuit.'

episode

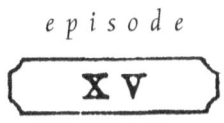

South Australian Register 15 May 1878

MURDERS AT PORT LINCOLN

On arriving in the magnificent harbour of Boston Bay the retiring Government Resident, Mr MacDonnell, met us on the beach, and informed us of the murder by natives of Mr John Brown, who was formerly in the service of the South Australian Company, and had latterly been a shipowner in the Port Lincoln district. This news greatly saddened us, especially as a short time earlier a lad named Hawson had also been speared by members of one of the tribes in the immediate neighbourhood of the settlement.

Poor Francis Hawson was speared on 5th October 1840. The facts connected with this incident prove that up to that date the conduct of the natives must have been inoffensive indeed. The boy was only twelve years of age, yet he was left alone in charge of sheep, and possessed food supplies most inviting to hungry or greedy savages, from whom his roughly constructed log hut would have offered very little protection. Early in the day a party of about a dozen black men and boys called at the station, as was often their custom. They invited little Frank to join them in hunting kangaroos. He of course declined. Had he done otherwise there can be little doubt that his life would have been saved, although the provisions or a substantial portion of them would have been stolen. The natives then asked for food, and he gave them flour and rice and a lighted stick with which to kindle a fire. In the hut was a sword and a gun. They asked for the latter, which he refused to give up to them. They next demanded to enter the hut, which demand he also refused to comply with. Closing the door, he placed himself, armed, on the outside of the hut. Two spears were thrown at him, both of which penetrated his chest. He then fired, and hit one of his assailants; the whole group of blacks then ran away. The spears remained in his body until evening, when the arrival of one of his brothers relieved his solitude. He was then trying to rid himself of the external portions of the spears by burning them in a fire, which he had managed to maintain by refuelling. The jagged heads of the spears could not be withdrawn, but his brother in some way relieved him by cutting away the external parts as near to the flesh as possible. He was supported on horseback by his brother and taken to the Port Lincoln settlement, where in those early days no surgical aid was obtainable, and after six days of extreme agony he died.

No other such encounter occurred until 2nd March, 1842, when Mr John Brown and his hutkeeper, a youth named Joseph Lovelock, fell victim to the natives. Towards sundown the shepherd was driving his flock in the direction of the hut, which was situated in a small valley, and could not be seen until approached quite closely. When at the distance of about a mile, the sheepdog, leaving the flock, stole towards the shepherd, crouched as if deeply dejected, and uttered a long dreary howl. This demonstration of his canine companion surprised the shepherd, and his surprise was increased when he observed that the flock, instead of proceeding steadily to their fold as usual, halted on the edge of a small watercourse which lay in their path, and resisted all efforts to make them advance. On looking into the cause he found a small pool of blood, from which the poor animals recoiled. On searching further he found Mr Brown stretched lifeless on his back, his head beaten in with waddies and his body covered with spear wounds. Near him were numerous impressions of naked feet and other indications of the murder having been carried out by natives.

The shepherd, scarcely knowing how to proceed, left the flock in the charge of his dog, and visited the hut. The door and window were open, and the fowls, finding this an opportunity to improve their quarters, were making roosting perches of the table and chairs. He called aloud several times, hoping to make the hutkeeper hear; but no answer was returned, except echoes of his own voice from the surrounding hills. He found the storeroom wide open, the flour removed, and articles not yet prized by the natives – tea for instance – scattered on the floor. He then proceeded to the nearest station for help, and the hutkeeper from there accompanied him back. Poor Lovelock was not to be found.

Four days elapsed before Lovelock's body was discovered. The police found it within one hundred yards of the hut, in a dry hollow of the creek bed. The stench caused by decomposition was then the cause of the discovery. Careful examination of the locality suggested that the boy had run from the back of the hut and fought his way to the spot where the body was discovered. Five yards from the hut was a broken spear, and about twenty yards further, in the same direction, Lovelock's musket, the contents of which had been discharged. The stock was broken. Beside the body lay Lovelock's pistol. It still retained the charge, but he had obviously attempted to fire it, for the hammer was down, the cap having exploded ineffectually without having ignited the main charge.

But little more than three weeks after the foregoing event, on the 29th of the same month, occurred the yet more disastrous and extensive tragedy which involved Mr Charles Biddle and his servants in its horrors. Mr Biddle's station was situated a few miles further from the Port Lincoln settlement than that of Mr Brown. The attack was made at noon, when Mr Biddle, a man named Fastins, and an old married couple of the name of Tubbs were together in the hut. All were killed except the old man, Charles Tubbs, who was left apparently dead, but as if by a miracle, recovered, and later returned to England. When I arrived at Port Lincoln the second time to assume my official duties in the settlement, Tubbs was still recovering from the attack and was to me an object of considerable interest. Besides many body wounds, which caused him great uneasiness, the injuries inflicted on him had rendered him virtually blind. A spear had been driven into his left eye, which not only destroyed the sight of it, but also produced sympathetic action on the right eye, and rendered it almost as useless for the purposes of vision. He must have been a calm, brave old man. Again and again he related to me, in my cottage, substantial details of the occurrence, so simply, graphically, and unostentatiously, that I have often since regretted I did not commit his narrative to paper in his own words, although I expect the sight of writing materials would have frozen at its source the unaffected stream of pathos which, unchilled by such influences, he poured forth copiously and without reserve. The substance and incidents of his narrative I am fortunately enabled to give as follows.

Natives had been observed loitering about the hut a day or two before, and the reflection of fires and sounds of corroboree at night indicated that large numbers had congregated in the neighbourhood. Probably the success of their attack on Brown's station prompted the yet more daring assault on that of Mr Biddle. The assailants chose the dinner hour on the latter occasion – exactly that time when the whole defensive force, except the shepherds, was gathered in the hut. Fastins, who was a powerful young man, went out of the hut to the assembled natives, hoping to conciliate them. He was received with a

EPISODE XV

shower of spears, and returned into the hut. He again went out, and threw a loaf of bread and a quantity of potatoes towards them. They immediately snatched up the eatables and retired long enough to consume them. No doubt they were convinced that everything else would also be yielded if they persevered, for, after the lapse of an hour, some forty of them returned. The three Englishmen arranged themselves outside. The natives then surrounded the hut and flung a shower of spears. One of these penetrated the leg of Fastins. Mr Biddle spontaneously fired a pistol at the assailants. There then arose loud yells of anger from the natives, who drew closer to the hut on all sides. The white men re-entered their frail fortress, and barricaded it to the inadequate extent which their means allowed. The blacks now made a breach in the wall, through which they poured incessant volleys of spears. Fastins attempted to discharge his gun, but it misfired. Mr Biddle fired a second pistol, as the natives rushed in. They filled the hut, and by mere physical pressure forced the four Europeans down. So densely packed were the blacks immediately after their entrance that old Tubbs, in the evidence that he gave at the Court House, said that 'the hut appeared filled with spears'. The work of slaughter now commenced, and proceeded at the will of the conquerors. Resistance was thenceforth useless. For as long as they were able each victim withdrew the numerous spears that penetrated him. Old Mrs Tubbs crept under the bed, hoping to escape molestation. At that same moment a spear struck Mr Biddle in the breast. He uttered one exclamatory sentence and was dead. One of the assailants got possession of a pitchfork, with which he wounded Fastins in several parts of the body. The pain occasioned by that implement was so great that poor Fastins, unable to move, requested Tubbs to shoot him, pointing to a pistol which lay on the floor. He died in great torment. The blacks next removed the bed, and repeatedly wounded Mrs Tubbs with the torturing pitchfork, and also with a pair of sheep-shears. When the natives had finally retired, Mrs Tubbs observing that her husband, who had withdrawn no fewer than six spears from different parts of his body, appeared to have escaped a mortal wound, but feeling that her own recovery was hopeless, counselled him as to his future plans, and made him promise that he would return to England as soon as possible. This promise he fulfilled as soon as practicable, due to the financial assistance generously offered by Mr Biddle's relatives. It was just after the conclusion of Tubbs' conversation with his wife that another spear was thrown into the hut, which penetrated his left eye and caused him to fall into a state of insensibility resembling death. The blacks then departed, believing that they had completed the tragedy.

Several hours later, a little before sundown, Tubbs recovered consciousness. On investigating the awful scene around him he found that Fastins was quite dead; so was Mr Biddle; but life still lingered in his wife. A new horror presented itself. The fence had been set fire to, and the fire had just caught the thatched roof of the hut. The old man spent his remaining strength in tearing down a portion of the burning fence and managed to fill two pails with water and attempted to quell the flames. Finding that the latter could not be extinguished he drew the three bodies from the hut and laid them side by side beyond the reach of the fire. He then withdrew the remaining spears from the lifeless forms, and laid himself down beside that of his wife. When found at sunset by the shepherds who returned with their flocks he was so exhausted that he could give them no particulars of the sad occurrence, but succeeded in making them understand that he desired not to be left alone.

Two natives named Narrabie and Nultia were subsequently tried in Adelaide as participators in the murders, convicted, and executed on the site of the devastated homestead.[5] Others of the tribe were subjected to lesser punishments.

EPISODE XV

The convicted felons were under my close observation for several days - the term that elapsed between their arrival at the settlement as condemned criminals and their execution. They were brothers, and probably twins, so alike were they in features and figure, and although I could distinguish one from the other when both were present, I was puzzled, and unable at the sight of either singly to declare which prisoner stood before me. No human sculptor working with ebony could have produced two more exquisite miniatures of the human form, for they were very small. Their hands and feet especially were beautiful. That most important feature, or collection of features, the head, presented nothing repulsive or sanguinary. Their foreheads were well formed. Their chins finely chiselled, their teeth faultless as ivory, their large lustrous eyes, if they failed to express acquired intelligence, were nevertheless full of human feeling and pathetic meaning.

I had frequent conversations with them, and whenever we talked of their approaching doom, as we generally did, their eyes filled with tears. They were always calm and gentle in their demeanour. No indication of ferocity manifested itself from first to last, and I am certain it was no element of their nature. The statement they made to me I fully believe. It was one whose admissions justified their punishment without fixing on them any prominent responsibility in regard to the atrocity committed. They were neither the plotters nor active perpetrators of it, yet nevertheless implicated in the foul outrage in common with all their tribe. As often happens among men of lighter colour, the greater criminals escaped, while some of the less guilty suffered.

In my conversation with them on the subject of futurity I neither led nor drove them. My object was to ascertain their views of eternity, if indeed their minds had ever conceived the idea of an after existence. Although by this time I had acquired a very conversable amount of the native dialect through daily contact with the tribes, the nature of the subject rendered precise and accurate communication of ideas on either side exceedingly difficult. Nevertheless they spoke frankly and seriously, and I concluded that certainly apart from any ideas communicated by Europeans they believed in a future unending existence, and held crude notions of rewards to virtue and punishment to vice. The details, of course, were tinged by the ignorance and degradation of their race.

episode

South Australian Register 24 May 1878

RECONCILIATION OF TRIBES

A year or two after the murders of Messrs. Brown and Biddle and their servants, natives of the tribes located nearest to the settlement of Port Lincoln who were not implicated with the Battara or Gum Scrub tribe in those murders resumed their occasional visits, partially obtaining food the while by cutting wood and carrying water for the settlers. An unusual number of them were located in our little village on the day of which I write, some time in 1843 or 1844, perhaps not fewer than a hundred and fifty.

About an hour before they were seated in numerous groups between my cottage and the waters of Boston Bay. I was gazing in a meditative mood on the Bay and on the picturesque island which shelters it from Spencer's Gulf, when a sudden panic among the native populace before me arrested my attention. Almost simultaneously two or three men sprang from their seats, uttering a short quick cry, and seizing their spears as they rose. In a few seconds all the fires were deserted. Men, women, and children fled with the utmost haste in a direction opposite to that to which the gaze of the startled fugitives had been directed. On leaving the house and looking over my garden fence I beheld a scene abounding in both the grotesque and the mysterious. A double column of blacks, elaborately painted, carrying poised spears and marching in good order beneath nodding plumes, were descending one of the stony hills immediately behind my residence. They advanced at a quick walk – almost a run – and at every fifty yards or so stopped suddenly, formed a circle and, uttering as with one voice a wild piercing monotone, instantly reformed and resumed their march. Directing my family to keep within the house, with closed doors and windows, I walked at a rapid pace towards the strange visitors. I was still about an acre or so from the advancing body, when quick footsteps and similar shrill sounds almost directly behind me caused me to turn. These sounds proceeded from a second body of natives that had approached through a gully between the hills, and were now at my own door. Returning I perceived that they were strangers, but found that I was known to them by description, as they hailed me by means of a name which another tribe had conferred on me. The parties having met, they fell out of rank and laid down their weapons. So suddenly had they appeared that mine was nearly the only European family yet aware of their presence in the settlement. In a few minutes a friend and brother officer conversant with and influential over the friendly tribes joined me. I accompanied him to the bivouac, where he recognised several of the more notorious murderers, but the greater number were strangers even to him, and were probably visiting the settlement for the first time. Through his persuasion the tribes very unwillingly permitted me as well as himself to witness the extraordinary ceremony hereafter described.

In a few minutes the newcomers again took up their spears, and the friendly natives, as we called them by way of distinction, approached in single column, bearing branches of the eucalyptus instead of weapons, and accosted the strangers with three distinct shouts. Not a woman or child had been visible since the incursion was made. The shapeless daubs of paint on the bodies of the invaded indicated how hastily their toilet had been made. A considerable display of continuous wheeling and winding in a figure-of-eight formation ensued. When the sun had descended 'our natives', repeating the three shouts and flinging their branches into the air, retired to the further extremity of the township, about half a mile distant.

The scene that followed produced an indescribable feeling of anticipation and excitement within me. The strangers whom I accompanied and the more distant but familiar blacks simultaneously commenced marching towards each other in such directions that on effecting a junction the combined body described a semicircle. Each party during its progress set fire to the herbage and shrubs on either side, and these, being abundant in quantity and very dry, burned fiercely and vividly irradiated the night. I shall not readily forget the effect produced by the continually multiplying flashes of pale and red light on the wild scenery around, and on the weird and wilder forms of the plumed and painted savages among whom I walked. Those settlers who beheld the exciting proceedings from distant heights subsequently told me that during their occurrence they conceived a very vivid idea of Pandemonium. I confess that a slight tinge of the trepidation mingled with my feelings as I gazed for the first time under such circumstances on the features of men whose very names, identified as they were with deeds of blood, had become so feared by shepherds and hutkeepers in the solitary bush. The march was accompanied by predetermined discordant yells and shouts and by the frequent clash of waddies that at intervals were brought into violent collision with one another.

On reaching a small open dell, about midway between the starting-points of the two parties, the stranger-blacks seated themselves in semicircular ranks on the side from whence they had arrived. About two minutes later the other column took their seats in similar order on the opposite side of the open space.

A multitude of 'bullroarers' – which was the name given by white-fellows to a crude and somewhat mysterious instrument used by the blacks – were swung round with unusual vehemence. This deafening device was a hollow piece of wood attached to a string, which was fastened to a stick. When whirled vigorously it exercised a thousand humming-top power and a chorus of them might be heard at a distance of many miles. The broad streaks of fire met; shrubs and trees which existed in unusual density near the rendezvous. They hissed and roared and crackled and shot forth columns of white light far more intense than that of day. Three youthful warriors from either party advanced to the centre of the circle and divested themselves of the skins that were their garments. These were rolled in bundles of three and secured with kangaroo sinews. Then two of the six, who wore thin bands of fabric around the neck and waist, knelt and clasped each other like wrestlers, whereupon two others from behind, passed the skins rapidly between the bodies of the clinging youths, and almost imperceptibly exchanged them. The equivalent bundles having been respectively handed to a senior warrior of either faction, the ceremony was concluded. Shouting and clashing of weapons were resumed for a few minutes, then both parties mingled in indiscriminate groups, and at length retired to their several encampments, but not to rest, as I know from woeful experience, for both sides encamped close to my cottage, and kept me awake till morning with their laughter and jabbering.

Soon after sunrise some injudiciously kind individual awakened me to witness a short series of duels, for although general matters were arranged it appeared that a few 'affairs of honour' were required to be disposed of. Never was there a more gentlemanly display in the rules of duelling. Two pairs of combatants exchanged some dozen or score spears, which were admirably thrown, but as adroitly parried, unmolested by the absurd intervention of seconds; but getting tired of the exercise they postponed the settlement of the quarrel to another opportunity. A third affair ended with more decisive result. An ebony coloured acquaintance of mine received his antagonist's spear in his left side, and for some time the wound threatened to be fatal. With our medical officer, Dr Harvey, having very recently died, I had the honour to undertake the case, which resulted in recovery. The reasons for the dispute between the combatants were as little illustrated by the encounter as they probably would have been in the case of white duellists.

I believe the ceremony of exchanging garments to have been significant of reconciliation. Much animosity had existed since the time of the murders between the guilty tribe and that which supplied information of their delinquencies. The object of the strangers was probably to settle the differences by a pitched battle. The boughs substituted for spears by the less warlike party were probably intended to operate as flags of truce, the exchange of skins as an emblem of renewed friendship, while the burning bushes, shouts, and clash of arms might be the equivalent, in a more civilised community, to a celebratory salute and ringing of bells and an illumination.

I offer the foregoing as my solution of the problem. The natives as usual in such cases made as much mystery about the matter as possible. One cross-grained old black, who had most wholeheartedly opposed my being present, took me by the coat several times during our fiery journey, and enforced with the greatest vehemence the absolute necessity for my secrecy. When his excessive attempts to intimidate me failed to have their desired effect he was horror-stricken, and informed me that if ever I acquainted a native woman of what I had seen her life would be sacrificed. In a spirit of mischief, and partly from curiosity, the next day I pretended to be going to speak to some of the females on the subject, but all of them shunned and fled from me as they would have done from a flying spear. I found that death really was the penalty for either seeing or talking of this and other peculiar observances of the males. No wonder, then, that all women and children were invisible during the ceremony of reconciliation, or whatever it may have been.

episode

XVII

South Australian Register 29 May 1878

PREHISTORIC
COLONIAL SCENES

Long before South Australia became the abode of a settled community its mainland and islands, in common with other portions of our island-continent, were occasionally visited and in some instances randomly settled on by human beings of a nomadic nature and a disposition or circumstance that longed for solitude. During the early part of the present century (1800s) many such men pursued a Robinson Crusoe sort of life on the islands with which Spencer's Gulf is studded.

These men were usually deserters from ships; convicts escaped from the penal settlements in New South Wales or Van Diemen's Land which colonies were at that time still the receptacles of heavily sentenced criminals from Great Britain; or wayward, eccentric, or unfortunate individuals who had voluntarily adopted that mode of life. The vagabond-like existence pursued by these men, however rugged it was, may readily be contemplated as free from privation and suffering, with a genial though occasionally over ardent climate, the seas, gulfs, and bays abounding with aquatic life of nutritive quality and excellent flavour. The mainland and islands bore edible roots and were inhabited by animals and birds, both large and small, possessing every quality necessary to sustain human life, hence starvation was not a contingency to be apprehended. Occasionally whaling vessels came into Boston Bay, not in search of whales, although within my recollection mountains of blubber have been captured there, but to take on water and to rest their crews. Of course these vessels carried with them such comforts as biscuit, tea, sugar, rice, tobacco, and spirits. These were made available via barter to the amphibious recluses about whom I am writing, for besides satisfying personal wants, they preserved the skins of seals and furry quadrupeds, collected shells of the nautilus and other inhabitants of the deep, branches of coral, sponges, &c., salted and smoked the bodies of wild geese and other waterfowl, and pursued a few other similar industries, so that when a whaler arrived at the anchorage they had the wherewithal to obtain comforts in exchange for their commodities. One of their most peculiar harvests was derived from the muttonbirds, whose scientific name I have for the moment forgotten. This extraordinary bird is about the size of a pigeon, and its egg rivals in size that of a goose. The latter, when boiled, I have eaten with a relish; but fried with bacon or absorbed into the composite of a batter pudding, it is exceptionable. The flesh of these birds, when properly prepared and cured, is delicious. Its flavour is a slight improvement on that of the genuine Yarmouth bloater [English herring]. A special characteristic of these strange birds is that on the same day of the same month, with a punctuality which would astonish and gladden a banker in commercially critical times, they habitually proceed to the islands in Spencer's Gulf in prodigious numbers, and there deposit their enormous eggs.

When I proceeded to Port Lincoln in March 1842, in the service of Government, many of these veteran haunters of solitude still existed. Of three chief varieties I sketched portraits with whatever photographic power I possessed; and although they are framed in verse – a form distasteful to the present practical and somewhat prosaic age – I present them as written, because they faithfully depict a phase of colonial life that has now become obsolete:

The Egg-gatherer

Along this shipless gulf, small rocky isles,
Like rugged warts, grow out of ocean's breast,
Where seals in sunshine climb and bask and rest
And unmolested snakes need not their wiles;
Myriads of sea-birds, in unending files,
O'ercloud them; each, in season, one vast nest
Egg-paven; then of brittle heaps in quest
Comes one bred mid hoares London's stately piles –
A homeless, sun-brown'd, weather-hardened man,
Plucking his meals from rocks and waves alone;
The human visage he doth rarely scan,
And save his boat, companion knoweth none;
His own purveyor; his own artisan;
One wayward will his law – even his own.

The Sealer

With thin-patched garb and shaggy visage sleeps
The weary sealer on that mossy ledge;
His drooping foot the wave's encroaching edge
Laves idly; overhead, clasped foliage keeps
Hot noon aloof – a mangrove screen, that weeps
Heart-shapen tears upon the watery floor,
Whence in arcades the trunks rise sheer and bare.
Shuddering with sudden chill, the faint breeze creeps,
And the sun-shunning fly twangs loud his horn
Within this lonely palace of the sea.
Part of the desert, though of woman born –
A human crag – most soundly slumbers he,

The sealer; one whose years have onward worn,
Dimless as waves in their monotony.

The Escaped Convict

Men are there whom, if we should chance to meet,
Guiding the team, or chasing through the deep
The whale, or on the hillside tending sheep,
Or moving with the throng in mart or street,
In townsmen's garb, or seaman's fashion neat,
Or bushman's wide-brim, woollen shirt, a belt –
We know – their caste less seen perchance than felt.
Hither comes one, whose lately fetter'd feet
Slid from their bonds, the fact lours through his smile;
A fix'd gaze on his heart wild tremors' rolls;
Of capture, and of chains, he thinks the while!
Crime ever holds whom he first cajoles;
And though his serfs cast prison-garments vile,
They cannot tear his livery from their souls.

What wonder if these men were as rugged as the scene around them! There can be no doubt that at the commencement of the present century many a tragedy was enacted in the neighbourhood of which I am writing, unheard of and perhaps unwitnessed by man. What was there to prevent men, perhaps naturally vicious, guided by no principle, restrained by no law, from shedding the blood of weaker or unarmed comrades in anger, revenge, or to obtain a paltry booty? Their outrages on natives, when they could inflict them with impunity, were undoubtedly many. Often at Port Lincoln, while sitting amid a tribe of aboriginals around their evening fire, have I heard from the elder members thrilling and repulsive narratives, the accuracy of which I had no reason to doubt. It is certain that island desperadoes occasionally visited the mainland, carried off native women by force, and murdered the children with whom their captives might unfortunately be encumbered.

About three-quarters of a mile from the dwelling which I occupied at Port Lincoln is, or was, a waterhole situated in the midst of a thin scrub, which deserved a far more gentle name, for it consisted of an immense variety of small flowering shrubs, whose blossoms, presenting every tinge of colour, were in many instances really beautiful. The narrow grassy avenues by which these natural shrubberies were intersected were thickly studded with the starry white and delicate blue flowers so prevalent in the uncultivated portions of the colony, as well as with the beautiful little fringe flower.

I am not certain that I was correct in using the term 'waterhole', which, I believe, usually designates a spring; for the small reservoir of which I speak was simply a deep round basin, sunk, I know not how, in a massive block of granite, and was so situated that every shower of rain assisted to replenish its store of water. I discovered it one day while waiting with my gun for an interview with a most interesting but shy family of wild turkeys who were accustomed on afternoons to wander in that direction. After having passed the spot scores of times without realising its existence, I suddenly stumbled upon it. Thereafter, I revisited the spot quite frequently. One fact however, struck me as being unusual. While bronze-wing pigeons, ground-parrots, parroquets, and many other birds fluttered over its surface and took a passing sip, and the smaller indigenous quadrupeds, when it was full of water, drank at its brink, no human native approached it, although the tribes availed themselves of an inconvenient and far inferior waterhole some distance away. That they had formerly been accustomed to slake their thirst at the granite basin was evident, for the trace of a 'native path' was still unobliterated.

On making enquiry I ascertained that the tribes superstitiously avoided the spot in consequence of a tragedy which had been enacted there some twenty years before. One day at that remote period a large party, consisting chiefly of lubras and piccaninnies who had concluded the morning forage, were seated around the shrub-screened waterhole. Several varieties of roots were slowly cooking in hot ashes; a few girls with bark cradles were dexterously sifting pupae of the large ant, so as to eject the least savoury and nutritious portions; while on the glowing embers fish, birds, wallaby, snakes, and goannas were undergoing various degrees of preparation for the anticipated meal.

In the meantime, unperceived by the dark skinned assembly, a small boat had rounded the southern extremity of Kirton Point, from which three white men landed, and, stealing under cover of the fragrant scrub, surprised the reclining party, shot some of the black men, and, before the scattered remainder had time to rally, bore off two women and conveyed them to an island a considerable distance away.

When I left the western portion of the colony, more than thirty years ago, the deep impression which had been made by this occurrence was beginning to subside, and the superstitious apprehension connected with the spot had been so overcome that some of the younger natives occasionally refreshed themselves at the scene of former violence and tragedy. To an outrage similar to that just narrated I am indebted for the subject of the ensuing episode of my Recollections, which I propose to designate – 'A Human Conundrum'. I have indulged somewhat freely in psychological studies, in prisons and elsewhere, but was never brought into contact with so strangely amusing a specimen of humanity as Bill Brien, of whom more anon.

episode

XVIII

South Australian Register 6 June 1878

BILL BRIEN, A HUMAN ENIGMA

An outrage similar to that described in my last episode is responsible for the anomalous position of the individual whom I have designated a human enigma. It has been said, time and time again, that if an Englishman or a Scotsman were to be born and raised in Ireland, he would display all the characteristics of an Irishman, and the following narrative proves that aborigines of Australia would under the same circumstances exhibit similar mental phenomena.

The most unusual mortal who is the subject of this article acquired his very limited knowledge of men and things on the almost desert island named after the enterprising Matthew Flinders. A year or two before the occurrence near Kirton Point which I have already narrated, a native of the Emerald Isle named Brien made a raid on the mainland, and carried off a female aboriginal to share his primitive habitat on Flinders Island, of which territory he had appointed himself monarch. The woman had with her a son, then about twelve months old. Brien was, according to custom, about to kill the boy, but the emotional pleas of the mother on this occasion prevailed and he said 'as he had stolen the dam he would preserve the cub'.

In a few years Bill (the name conferred on him by his abductor) became very useful to Brien. He could handle an oar, help to capture a seal, discharge a rifle with precision, and execute any manual labour with the efficiency of a youth born in Europe. His habits, of course, became those of his teacher, and the few ideas he managed to acquire were derived from the same source. In the occasional absence of the old sealer he was not a bad hand at bartering skins, melons, etc. for garments, tobacco, spirits, and a few other 'notions', with whale-ships cruising in the neighbourhood. His own language he never knew, and even his mother after a few years forgot it, but instead he imbibed the rich brogue of old Brien.

When I had the honour to make his acquaintance Bill had seen no aboriginal inhabitant of South Australia other than his mother, and but few white people except Brien and the whalers. Until the period of which I write he had never left Flinders Island. It was in the autumn of 1845 that he favoured me with a visit. I was then dwelling alone in an isolated cottage close to the margin of Boston Bay. On hearing the greeting, 'How do you do?' and raising my head from the pages of a book which I was perusing, I was not a little surprised to see before me a strapping blackfellow, six feet high, clad in a sailor's jacket, blue stripe shirt, moleskin trousers, a round straw hat, and provided, moreover, with a double barrel gun and a short black pipe. Without waiting for an invitation he grounded his gun, seated himself, and began to cut tobacco, looking the while inquisitively over the apartment, and seeming to be especially puzzled by the books that were lying about.

What is he? Where does he come from? were the first thoughts that suggested themselves to my mind. He was an animated conundrum. His features and colour were those of an Australian aboriginal, his garb and equipment bespoke a bushman, and his dialect was the English commonly spoken by the peasantry of Ireland.

'Where did you come from?' I asked.

'From Flinders Island,' was the reply.
'What countryman are you?'
'An Irishman.'
'What's your father's name?'
'He's dead – died two months ago.'
'But what's his name?'
'Sure he told me it was Brien.'
'And what is your name?'
'Bill Brien.'
'Are there any more of you?'
'Yes, I have two sisters and mother on the island.'

He then informed me in what manner and with whom he left the island, and became very talkative and inquisitive.

'Does nobody live here with you?' he asked, and observed that before entering he thought the house was uninhabited 'it looked so lonesome like'. He had probably never seen gold, for observing my watch on the table he remarked, 'That's a handsome watch – what a beautiful colour!'

He was apparently not accustomed to see much money of any sort; for, speaking of an island trader known to both of us, he said, 'That man Andrews is worth an immense deal of money.'

'Where does he keep it?' I asked.
'Mostly on Middle Island.'
'How much do you think he is worth?'
'I don't rightly know – I was never told.'
'How much do you *think* he is worth?'
'Oh, an immense deal. I dare say three or four pounds in all.'

On many subjects my questions produced great confusion of ideas, and his very identity seemed entwined with that of old Brien. 'Would you like to see Ireland?' I asked.

The answer was – 'Yes, faith and sure I just would now; I'd like to see the old country once more before I die.'

His first interview with his own countrymen amused me

excessively. I had the honour to introduce him to them. The primitive natives were seated in groups among sandhills, and on my approach with the dark stranger, of whose arrival in Boston Bay they knew long before the fact was known to white men, they became silent, but assumed an appearance of perfect indifference. Bill observed equal silence. He looked on them at first with an air of patronising dignity, yet sufficiently guarded to repel familiarity, and he evidently never forgot the vast difference subsisting even between an amateur white man and a blackfellow. The natives, one and all, cast upwards indescribable glances, indicating distrust, dislike, contempt, and probably half a dozen other kindred feelings. I introduced him as a brother native; but they denied the implication, and disputed my statement with such triumphant queries as the following: 'Why can he not speak our language?' 'Why is he not tattooed in keeping with tribal custom?' 'How is it that he uses a gun instead of a spear?' I asked 'Is he then a white man?' To which they replied in effect, in a dialogue consisting of about equal portions of English and native, 'Why not? Since he lives with you, speaks your tongue, wears your dress, and uses your weapons?' Then, with scornful expressions of countenance and angry intonation, they summed up by declaring 'He is neither a white man nor a black man,' and added in pure English, 'he is no good.' Bill on the other hand, being asked after the interview what he thought of his countrymen, replied, 'Oh, they are dirty brutes!' and added, 'I don't like blackfellows – they are a dirty lazy set!'

One day I noticed that Bill was unusually merry. The fact was a cask of Cape wine had arrived at the settlement, an incident that occurred usually about twice a year, and Bill had imprudently sampled a good portion of it. He capered, howled, whistled, handled a shillelagh with an air that would have done credit to Donnybrook; sang 'St Patrick was a jintlemon' and 'Kitty of Coleraine', told interminable and incomprehensible stories about 'owld Ireland', and towards sundown subsided into a leaden slumber in the outhouse, which was his appointed dormitory. The rest to which his vocal and gymnastic efforts had fully entitled him, he was not permitted to enjoy. His lighter complexioned companions of the day who of course were far more advanced in the ways of civilisation, and consequently more accustomed to drinking alcohol, determined to conclude the evening's diversion with a cruel interruption of poor Bill's slumber. Having in vain attempted to awaken him by ordinary means they surrounded the partly open shed in which he reclined and favoured him with a serenade composed of every inhuman sound of which the human voice is capable. To provide appropriate instrumental accompaniments for the vocal performance they utilised shovels, iron kettles, porter bottles, whip-whistles, corn measures and an old speaking trumpet. None but an inhabitant of the grave could have remained deaf to this. Bill partly raised himself in utter amazement and rubbed his eyes as if imploring those organs, although the night was intensely dark, to explain the mystification in which his ears were involved. Then, sundry lucifers ignited in quick succession, every match being discarded when the blue flame was about to give place to one of a paler and more enlightening colour. The poor blackfellow, open-eyed, open-mouthed, and shaking with terror, demanded what was the matter. Then one of the conspirators, mimicking the voice and the broad Irish accent of old Brien, who had died but two months before, asked in a hoarse, angry and yet unnatural voice. 'Bill, you wretched lad, how is it that the moment I'm laid beneath the sod you leave your sisters and your own born mother and the pigs and the garden crops and the smuggled whisky, and all the family chattels to be carried away by the sealers, or the American whalers, or anybody else that pleases? There's the hut burnt down – your mother and sisters are murdered to death – the pigs have eaten up the wheat – and I can't sleep in my grave – while you are here, you ungrateful and uncaring scoundrel, singing and dancing and drinking as if I had never gone dead at all, at all!'

During this awful address poor Bill sprang to his feet, trembled like a blancmange when first touched by the spoon, blubbered and at intervals exclaimed – 'Go back, go back, father dear, to the neat little grave where we laid ye; go back at once to the island, and I'll be there before ye!'

The abjectness of Bill's terror, his imploring and apologetic blarney and the strange attitudes which he unconsciously assumed created a burst of laughter which made him aware of the hoax that had been practised on him. But regardless of his knowledge of the deception, and the perfect sobriety which excessive fear had produced, poor Bill would not sleep alone during the remainder of the night.

episode

XIX

South Australian Register 26 June 1878

SETTLING DOWN IN A NEW TOWN

I returned to Adelaide with the dismal tidings of the murder of Mr Brown and his hutkeeper. A few days after my arrival a whaleboat delivered an official communication to Adelaide advising that Mr Biddle and his servants had also been murdered. The matter had assumed a decidedly serious aspect. Some mounted troopers were promptly assigned to reinforce the local police, and a party of the 96th Regiment, under the command of Lieutenant Hugonin, was dispatched to the scene of the murders. We were hurried away with all possible expedition.

The vessel, although a trifle larger than the regular trader, was very small, and passengers, soldiers, luggage, furniture, and merchandise were crammed into her interior after a most haphazard and uncomfortable fashion. Personally, I fared admirably on some sacks of flour; nevertheless five days and nights of this situation was amply sufficient. The weather was boisterous and the water rough, for several antagonistic currents sometimes set in among the numerous little islands which stud Spencer's Gulf, and give a small sailing vessel a motion or combination of motions far more unpleasant than either pitching or rolling. On this occasion our tub tumbled about very much as an intoxicated porpoise might be expected to do. To attempt a stroll on deck was to risk being flung over the extremely low bulwarks;

and if the hot iron chimney of the caboose were caught hold of for security, it was a support which could not be clung to for long.

We entered Boston Bay after nightfall. The houses forming the settlement were all within sight of the vessel, having been built at intervals along the curve of the shore for about a mile, yet at so early an hour as eight o'clock not a light was visible. This was strange. The night was too dark for the inhabitants to have dispensed with lamps or candles; and the hour was too early to favour the idea that all had retired to rest Clouds over the mainland a few miles off gave back reflections from innumerable native camp fires. We could not resist the passing thought, 'Did the blacks muster their whole strength and slaughter the entire village?'

Lieutenant Hugonin landed with his redcoats, and most of the male passengers accompanied them. When I first visited the Bay I occupied an extensive wooden house of English manufacture which had been erected on the seabeach by Captain Porter, who was one of the earliest settlers. I at once proceeded to the cottage, ascended the steps and knocked at the door. This I did several times, but elicited no answer except echoes from the empty rooms. I walked round to the back of the house, but could discern no indication of life within, although on sailing three weeks before I had left it in the charge of a steady married couple. At length I heard footsteps. The old housekeeper, who had been greatly scared by the noises I made, had caught a glimpse of me in the twilight, and became quite courageous when informed of the arrival of the military. A reason for the sepulchral appearance of the settlement was given. During the last fortnight masses of natives had been so numerous and their demeanour so threatening that the windows of every house had been barricaded outside with boards placed as closely together as practicable. These were all knocked off the morning after we arrived.

EPISODE XIX

That same morning not a native could be found within many miles of the settlement. The departure of the military and police in pursuit of them afforded me an opportunity of reinspecting the beauties and investigating the peculiarities of my locality. When I looked on that noble expanse of sheltered water known as Boston Bay – a name bestowed on it by explorer Matthew Flinders – I was not surprised that some of the earlier settlers were desirous of fixing the seat of government there. Such a measure, however would have proved very unfortunate for the colony. When a few months later the Governor visited the settlement and witnessed the sterile character of the back country, Captain Grey observed that, had Boston Bay occupied the site of Holdfast Bay, South Australia as a colony would have possessed pre-eminent natural advantages.

Among other interesting phenomena Boston Bay possessed below high-water mark a spring of deliciously fresh and cold water. It was situated at the then northern extremity of the settlement in front of the entrance to Happy Valley. During a considerable portion of each day the briny waters of the Gulf absorbed and contaminated the purity of the spring, but when the tide was low it gushed up sparkling into the merry sunshine, much to the delight and refreshment of innumerable bipeds and quadrupeds which anxiously awaited its periodical emancipation. As the tide was receding it was curious to watch the sturdy little spring bubbling up and battling with the yielding ripple of salt water. Within a few minutes it was as free from salt as a mountain rill. Often on a warm afternoon have I laid down my double-barrel and generally heavy game-bag and waited, pannikin in hand, for a draught of the cold, crystal clear liquid. I always satiated my thirst promptly, for many thirsty creatures were waiting their turn whom shyness or fear prevented from forestalling me. In long continued dry weather I have seen neighbouring trees and bushes thronged with bronze-wing pigeons, parrots, and other birds watching the receding tide, while wallaby and other small quadrupeds, and sometimes even the kangaroo and emu, would bide their time in some thicket. Horses and cows also grazing in the neighbourhood would punctually attend the rendezvous. The fact that most surprised me was the accurate knowledge that this very assorted assemblage of quadrupeds and bipeds appeared to possess of the flowing and receding tide. I never saw any of them waiting at or near high water.

So considerable was the water thrown up by this small fountain that on one occasion three large whalers replenished their stocks of water from it before returning to their fishing grounds; and this was effected in two days, although the spring was only available a few hours each day. A remarkable result of this enormous drain on its resources was that it disappeared. In a few days I found that it had only changed its place, having moved to a few yards distant from the old site and a trifle further from high-water mark.

Near to the entrance to Happy Valley, and consequently to the submarine spring, stood the residence of Dr Harvey, our medical officer. I will narrate three interesting but painful incidents that within a very short space of time occurred there. Dr Harvey had in his service a young couple named Rush, who resided in a cottage adjacent to the doctor's dwelling. The two houses were situated on a tall cliff overhanging Boston Bay, and the island of the same name by which for ten miles the bay is landlocked on the eastern side. The Rushes had a little girl about two years old. When last seen the child was playing in front of the cottage on the cliff against the base of which at high water the sea washed. Only a few minutes later she was missed, called for, searched for, but was never seen again, either alive or as a corpse. Not a fragment of her skeleton, not a tatter of her dress, was ever recovered. Not an exclamation of alarm, not a cry of

EPISODE XIX

pain, indicated the moment of her exit from human knowledge. No bruised herbage, no lacerated soil, no strange footprint of man or beast indicated where the child had disappeared. The most probable surmise was that she had fallen over the cliff. Had she done so when the tide was in, a receding wave might have conducted her to the jaws of a shark; but on the contrary, the disappearance occurred at low water. The body was not on the beach, nor did the sand exhibit any trace of it. Of natives there were none in town, and had one of them been guilty of abduction the fact would certainly have oozed out. All was mystery, and although the incident occurred thirty-five years ago the mystery retains its original density.

Dr Harvey died suddenly and the settlement was left without medical aid for several months. This is a serious contingency to which distantly isolated settlements are subject. We were commonly two and not unfrequently three months without communication with Adelaide. Less than three months previously the death had occurred of Mrs Harvey, a most amiable and to some extent accomplished woman. Her health was extremely delicate. Death was evidently making his advances in that stealthy and repulsive form which is called consumption. Her tinted cheek and glistening eye, together with a very gradual yet noticeable weakening of frame and limb, attested the presence and the progress of the disease. Although her disease was gradual her death was sudden. One day, after dinner, she leaned back in her easy chair as she was accustomed to do for slumber, and remained unconscious a longer period than usual. It was found that she had commenced that sleep from which there is no awakening.

Dr Harvey had a garden on Boston Island at the back of a little fairy bay, on the velvet sand of which you might sometimes pick up the shell of a paper-nautilus without the loss of a splinter. It was a very pleasant sail from this residence to the island in summer time. One afternoon I was sitting there with Mrs Harvey on what she told me was her favourite musing spot. It was on the western side of a large and shady gum-tree, and commanded a view of the rippling waters of the bay, beyond which her own residence was visible backed by the undulating forest scenery of the mainland. It was a lovely and serene afternoon. Our conversation took a pensive and metaphysical direction, and during its continuance she informed me that the spot on which we sat had been chosen as her final resting place. Little did I think then that the spot would be so soon occupied by her. Shortly after this interlude I again crossed Boston Bay, this time in company with the Resident and other Government officers in the wake of Dr Harvey's boat, which contained the remains of his late wife. On visiting the grave at a later date, I penned the following sonnet, which I preluded by the title:

The Island Grave

Pining, she reached this shore, and our bland air
Upon her lovely cheek prolonged the smile,
And held his prey from grisly Death awhile.
The respite o'er, we, as she bade us, bore
Her clay to yon lone isle, and laid it where
Trees clustering shade the vale — a most sweet grave,
Reached by the moan of the surrounding wave,
Nought human else or lives or moulders there.
If viewless things the ranks of being swell —
Fairies or nymphs — upon that isle they dwell;
And there sometimes, perchance, her gentle soul doth brood,
Where beams, hues, odours, sounds, do ever meet,
From dawn till starlight dies, sweet chasing sweet,
And from man's cloudy world no shadow dares intrude.

EPISODE XIX

A spot of vast historical and general interest is Stamford Hill, situated opposite to the southern extremity of Boston Island, and forming one side of the southern entrance to the harbour. It is a bluff of substantial height and rises almost perpendicular. Indeed it is unascendable on all sides but one, and that one is sufficiently steep to challenge the fittest human muscles and joints, and lungs of the most leathern toughness, to the utmost. On the summit of that eminence in November, 1802 stood the great navigator Flinders, and at his side, then a midshipman, the subsequently great and much lamented northern explorer Franklin. They were probably the first Europeans who had beheld at one view the shores of Spencer's Gulf and the clusters of islands with which the Gulf is thickly studded. It became part of my official duty to ascend the hill twice, first to see a commemorative obelisk commenced, and second time to report on the completion of the work. On first reaching the summit, I was overawed with the living map which extended for many miles in all directions of sea and shores and islands; in fact I beheld the very scene which for the first time burst on the vision of Flinders and Franklin on the very day of my birth. The weather was unusually warm for Port Lincoln, but on the summit of the hill a thick cloak would have contributed greatly to my comfort.

The obelisk was built by order and at the expense of Lady Franklin, whose conjugal devotion induced her to scale the formidable Stamford Hill and gaze on the scene which had been witnessed by her heroic husband forty years before. The column is now a landmark visible in clear weather for many miles, but when first distinguished in extreme distance, although reaching a considerable altitude, it appears to be exceedingly small. Because the building stone of Port Lincoln is rather soft, Lady Franklin at considerable extra expense caused stone to be imported from Tasmania. The obelisk bears an inscription which was drawn up by Lady Franklin – a copy of which I took, but cannot readily find.

This instance of the wife's attachment to her then living but absent husband was quite in unison with subsequent acts of untiring devotedness, which deserve to hand her name down to posterity among the names of distinguished females whose conjugal heroism has cast lustre on their sex.

e p i s o d e

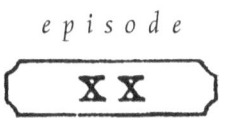

South Australian Register 3 July 1878

NATIVES IN THEIR PRIMITIVE CONDITION

My acquaintance with native tribes in Adelaide and its neighbourhood allowed me to see first hand, the state of squalor and degradation to which intercourse with vicious Europeans had reduced them. At Encounter Bay and in its immediate vicinities I first knew them to be industrious and untiring in useful and athletic pursuits, but their characters had been considerably eroded by long association with whalers, sealers, and other similar craftsmen. At Port Lincoln and in the country beyond it, on the contrary, I had communication with numerous tribes who were altogether uninfluenced by contact with Europeans, many of them never having beheld the countenance of a white man. Consequently, I could fairly estimate their characteristics in the normal condition. But before I proceed to this more pleasing task I must narrate another tragedy or two, and the catalogue of murders will close in the last episode of these Recollections with a circumstantial account of the assassination of Mr Charles Christian Dutton and his four companions.

In August 1844 Mr Darke, accompanied by Mr Theakstone, his second in command, with both of whom I had been long intimate, arrived at Port Lincoln, Mr Darke being commissioned to explore unknown country lying to the North-west of Port Lincoln. His youth and early manhood had been spent in

New South Wales and Tasmania. Many of his adventures in the bush of those countries were very remarkable, often exceedingly romantic. The thrilling narratives which he related to me evening after evening, as we sat together in the interval which preceded the commencement of his fatal expedition, related chiefly to escaped convicts, bushrangers, and other desperadoes. Some of these narratives were too horrible even to excite interest; they described lashing human beings to trees in the most scorching weather, smeared with some substance attractive to flies and other tormenting insects, then leaving them to perish by slow degrees; roasting men alive by a gradual process, commenced at the lower extremities; and other demoniac atrocities.

The explorers headed north from Port Lincoln and had no contact with natives for two months, but on 22nd October a party of them made their appearance. The explorers gave them presents of sugar, damper, and a few other articles. On the morning of the 23rd Mr Darke had occasion to walk a short distance from his party. He went alone and unarmed. A few minutes afterwards a cry of surprise or pain was heard from him, and the exclamation was followed by a shout from the natives. Theakstone and one of the men (the other being absent collecting the bullocks) rushed to the spot armed, and seeing a black in the act of hurling a spear, fired, but missed the spearman, who, with about twenty other natives, at once decamped. Darke was found prostrate and transfixed by three spears in the abdomen, hip, and knee respectively. His comrades succeeded in removing the weapons, but that fixed in the knee, being barbed, caused much agony and injury. The wounded man and his companions were greatly concerned for the safety of the bullock-driver, who was an unusually long time getting the animals together. The latter during the night had taken a new direction, and strayed to a longer distance than ever before. This

EPISODE XX

unusual circumstance was no doubt attributable to their knowledge, whether instinctive or sensitive; that blacks were approaching. Once when I was in the remote bush a team of oxen suddenly lifted up their heads, tossed and lashed their tails, and started at full speed in a particular direction. The teamster having rounded them up, pointed to the opposite quarter, and observed, 'Blacks are approaching.' The announcement proved to be correct, but at that time the tribe was still many miles away.

The crippled party now turned the heads of their team towards Port Lincoln. Mr Darke suffered great agony from the jolting of the dray, so a hammock was constructed, in which he was slung. He was very desirous of reaching, if not the settlement, the coast of the bay. His mind recoiled from the thought of being buried in that rugged savage wilderness. There, however, he was fated to die, for the next day mortification ensued, and he died before midnight. To convey the body to the settlement was impracticable; to reach the latter themselves was not an easy matter for the survivors. Fortunately they effected the latter object by forced marches, but in the process endured much anxiety, fatigue and thirst. Before leaving Darke's grave they burned the bush over it and in the immediate neighbourhood, so as to make the spot undistinguishable from the surrounding soil. No doubt the repugnance the deceased felt to being buried in the scrub arose partly from an apprehension of his remains being exhumed by natives.

For weeks before the fatal attack was known to have taken place, I felt certain that Darke or one of his party had been killed. Adjacent to my residence was a large outhouse that contained a fireplace, here natives, sometimes in groups of up to twenty, would spend the night. More than once I heard them discussing, as I believed, the death either of Mr Darke or Mr Theakstone. I endeavoured quietly to learn the facts, but without success.

The moment we began to interrogate natives on any subject which might implicate their own tribes or neighbouring tribes in dangerous responsibilities they would dissemble, mystify, and endeavour to explain away anything they had incautiously stated. To my rather close questioning some replied that they were talking of Biddle's murder, some that they were not alluding to 'kruckabucca' (dying) of a white man, but to a speared black-fellow, &c.

One day, having wandered a few miles from the settlement with my constant companion, a two-barrel rifle and fowling-piece on my arm, I suddenly met a bushman whom I at once knew to be Mr Theakstone. After a mutual exclamation and shake of the hand I asked, 'Where's Darke?' He took from his breast-pocket and handed to me a piece of wood about six inches long, with a barb at the pointed end like a fish-hook. This was the extremity of the spear that had caused Mr Darke's death, and the wood was deeply tainted with his blood. I walked back to the settlement with Theakstone.

The tragic occurrence just narrated was the last which occurred during my residence at Port Lincoln; but on my revisiting that spot a year or two after on matters connected with Mr Biddle's death I was surprised to meet Captain Beevor, who had headed the volunteer party which assisted to chastise the Milmenrura murderers of passengers from the *Maria*. We spent three pleasant evenings together, chatting of old colonial incidents, and by no means excluding our warfare with the aborigines. Shortly after one of the natives split open his head with an axe, stealthily approaching him while he was engaged in chopping firewood.

My purpose in this and the following episode of Recollections is to present a faithful portraiture, however incomplete it may be, of tribes of natives in their primitive condition which have now wholly passed away, or are represented by inconsiderable remnants whose original features have been obliterated or disturbed. After the gloomy catalogue of tragic incidents which I have narrated the reader of course will expect that the first characteristic of the native which required change was ferocity. But, strange to say, whatever may have been the cause of those murders, whether our aggression on their hunting grounds or individual provocation, I never detected a trace of ferocity in the composition of the Western native. As I found him before he came into contact with Europeans, he was a simple artless being, whose childhood continued to adult age. If weather was congenial and food abundant he was contented and happy, entering fully into the enjoyment of both. The thought of one changing to inclemency and the other becoming scarce never entered his brain. His life was 'today'. The past with him left no indelible record and was forgotten as rapidly as possible, and with the future he troubled himself very little indeed. It was contentment with the present and absence of forethought which chiefly kept him stationary from one generation to another.

His disposition was kind and genial, and he was courteous and frank in his demeanour. My first interview with individuals of a distant tribe, after the malevolence which had arisen between the black and white races due to the murders and acts of retribution, impressed me with this fact, and numerous subsequent instances abundantly confirmed it. It chanced one day, when the excitement of warfare had somewhat subsided, that I had walked a few miles from the settlement, and having found a small spring of water in a grassy hollow was seated beside it eating the sandwich which I had carried in my gamebag. The latter and my gun were laid beside me. While thus engaged I saw above the ridge of the hollow, moving towards me, or rather to the spring, the upper and pointed end of a spear, then another, and another. I thrust the uneaten portion of my meal into the bag, slung it over my shoulder, poised the gun on my arm, reached the level ground, and walked in the direction of the approaching natives. A few moments later I was confronted by five males previously unknown to me, who, after uttering the apparently involuntary exclamation 'heugh!' laid down their spear and waddies, called me by the name Port Lincoln natives had conferred on me, 'Obootoo', and advanced towards me with their right hands extended for the interchange of the British token of amity. Having laid down my gun and shaken hands with them successively, we sat down by the spring for some time. One of them gathered for me a sort of fruit which Europeans had named the 'wild strawberry', solely I suspect from the similarity of smell to the European fruit, for in no other respect was there any analogy. They were evidently pleased when I received and ate these vegetable lollies, and still more when I handed to each a fragment of my own repast. They accompanied me back to the settlement. Their demeanour throughout was friendly, yet fearless and unembarrassed.

I have often admired the confident, almost proud bearing of youthful warriors when I have met them marching in single file with long swift strides through their native forests, elaborately adorned with war paint. The head was then thrown back, the chest was dilated, and the waving emu feather which issued from a mass of flowing, glossy, raven-black hair, and was surmounted by a tapering and erectly poised spear, completed an aspect decidedly warlike. Much gentleness and playfulness have I witnessed among themselves and towards their children, and one continuous act of kindness towards old age greatly interested me. A tribe resident some seventy miles from the settlement had amongst them a patriarch who was apparently as antiquated as the mummies of Egypt. His trunk and limbs were shrunken almost to the dimensions of the mere bones, and had the appearance of dusky parchment. His hair was literally white as snow and would have formed a strange contrast to his skin

EPISODE XX

had not the latter been bleached to a pale brown. He was in a state of utter helplessness physically, but evidently retained intellect enough to share in the mirth of his tribe when matters were prosperous and to feel depression when the reverse occurred. He was constantly fed and tended in all respects as a child would be by his people, and whenever they changed their locality he was borne with them, sometimes on their shoulders, and at others with hands across, as two children occasionally in play carry a third child.

I asserted that I never detected ferocity as a characteristic of the Western tribe. It is true that they sometimes dealt injury inflicted by one white man, on others of his race; but this was in accordance with the system adopted towards themselves by the more enlightened palefaces. But although not, as far as I could detect, cruel, cold blooded, or malignant, they were undoubtably to a great degree, excitable, impulsive, and sometimes uncontrollable in their rage. I have seen them when thus excited hurl every disposable article within reach, fragile or otherwise, at an offending individual, even wrenching shrubs from the ground to utilise as weapons. In these fits of passion they would scream, tear their hair, cut their own flesh and assume bodily contortions befitting demons - dilated, fire-flashing eyes completing the hideous resemblance. I once saw a middle-aged woman who, after having had a long, high-pitched verbal battle with her husband, continued for the space of an hour in a condition of mental and physical tempest which on its subsidence left her for some time in a state of exhaustion which bordered on torpor.

episode

XXI

South Australian Register 10 July 1878

ADDITIONAL CHARACTERISTICS OF NATIVES

Strange as the statement I made in the preceding episode (that ferocity did not appear to be a constituent portion of the nature of the western aboriginal) may appear to the reader, I am prepared to go further, and to assert that I often observed indications of instinctive delicacy on the part of natives newly brought into contact with white people. In summer our doors in the daytime were constantly open, and it was natural that individual natives known to us who had just arrived from the bush, perhaps bearing a present of crayfish or gigantic mushrooms, should step directly in, as we did ourselves, but they never penetrated to an inner room; and if they found us busy, engaged with friends, or discussing a meal, they would immediately retire for a time. On my mentioning instances of this apparently incongruous conduct to the local Protector of Aboriginals, he said he also was familiar with such instances, and on my remarking that the characteristic might be described as natural politeness, he observed that his own language, German, would not supply an epithet more applicable.

A repulsive attribute of those begging natives who haunt inland towns is their extreme filthiness, yet I am far from convinced that there is any natural affinity between the race and dirt. At Port Lincoln I gave them credit for exemplary cleanliness. It may be argued that this cleanliness was the result of them living in close proximity to the bay, much of their time in summer being spent in the water; but I have seen a damper made by one of them that I would willingly have partaken of, the hands, and the stone on which the dough was mixed and kneaded, were so scrupulously clean, and any extraneous substance wafted to it by the wind, such as a leaf or flake of wood-ash was so carefully excluded that I could have eaten it with my usual relish. Once, when travelling, I enjoyed a fish after witnessing both the catching and the cooking of it by a native woman, who hospitably pressed it upon me. The whiting considerably improved the quality and flavour of my dinner, and probably the bread and salt which I gave in return added similarly to hers.

I have heard the natives accused of being completely without emotion or curiosity of any kind, but I do not think that this claim can in any way be justified. In the West I observed abundant instances of the exercise of intelligent curiosity. Their occasional voicelessness in the presence of white men I believe partly arises from self-restraint and partly from the fact that all things connected with the intruders are so strange to them that they fail to be excessively astonished at anything. I once tried to startle old Koongulta from his assumed warrior-like indifference. A cannon had to be discharged for the first time, and I placed the old man very close to the gun. Powder was not used sparingly. The result was a peal of thunder which was returned with interest from Boston Island and the hills at the back of the settlement. The unusual din startled thousands of seabirds from their fishing stations, but its only effect on Koongulta was to cause him to turn to the gunner with a smile and then to me with something which amounted to a self-conscious grin.

A mirror when first seen puzzled them considerably. On

beholding their own figures they would vary their attitudes, alter the expression of features, and apply their hands to the latter in various ways to assure themselves of the identity of the reflection.

Our communication with each other by writing occasioned them much unsatisfactory reflection. I was a most important personage in their estimation, because I made out the committals of such individuals as were set to Adelaide for trial. Some of them remonstrated earnestly with me on behalf of one man, who had been tried for and convicted of sheep stealing, assuring me that he was not guilty. 'Paper,' they said, in faltering English, 'very good; but that time make mistake.' The man's innocence was later made apparent, and he was released. The statements of the blacks on this occasion were very satisfactory, inasmuch as they proved that in other cases the guilty persons had been convicted. When he was at Port Lincoln Mr George French Angas sketched the figure of a supposed ringleader of the outrages which had been committed. At page 190 of 'Savage Life and Scenes', Mr Angas states:

> One of these men, Milliltie, who was marked out as having thrown one of the spears that killed young Hawson, being a remarkably wild looking fellow, I began sketching him; when he suddenly bolted, imagining that I was exercising some witchcraft over him by which his evil deeds might be discovered.

The fact was, after I had picked Milliltie out and placed him in position for the artist, he suspected that Mr Angas was about to make out his committal. I tried in vain to get him back; he exclaimed, 'No me do it! No paper! No go Adelaide!'

To illustrate their mystification in regard to writing the following anecdote will suffice. I possessed a large fish-kettle which I often lent to natives, who used it for boiling wheat. As the utensil was sometimes absent when I required it, I made a rule that it should never be lent but by myself or on my written order. One day, a few miles from the settlement, I met Utulta, who had been made a constable, and was accompanied by several natives who had not visited us before. He had wheat with him and requested the loan of the kettle. With my pencil I wrote on an envelope the required order. While I was thus occupied Utulta was telling his more ignorant countrymen what would be the result of my scribbling, which statement they received with evident incredulity. On my return home I found that he had handed in my pencil message without uttering a word, his companions meanwhile awaiting the result in silence. When the kettle appeared they shouted, laughed, jumped, rolled on the ground, and behaved in all respects more like maniacs than respectable gentlemen in black.

My reputation among the natives was greatly enhanced by having announced to them an eclipse of the sun twenty-four hours before its occurrence. Long before the time I had indicated a considerable number of them had assembled, among whom I distributed pieces of smoked glass as extensively as my stock of fractured crystal would permit. After a while they began to grow incredulous, and laughed good-naturedly at the supposed hoax; but when the lunar globe began to obscure the sun's disc they became much interested, shouting 'Minga! Minga!' – he is ill; and enquired if he [the sun] would 'kruckabucca' – die. That which surprised them was not the eclipse – they had witnessed such occurrences before – but the fact of my foreknowledge.

Stupidity is not a characteristic of the South Australian native. With favourable opportunities he learns to read and write with average facility and to pronounce the English language with equal correctness to European foreigners. A few of our letters, however, occasion them considerable trouble, none more than 'S'. I used to exercise a considerable number of them with the sentence 'sixty-six sovereigns six shillings and sixpence', and if the successive attempts of the grinning students did not result in much profit, they produced a copious fund of amusement as one after another spluttered out 'tickty-tick tov', &c., &c., each breaking down before the termination of the sentence, a chorus of laughter accompanying the failure.

I had frequent proof that the western aborigines were possessed even of fancy and imagination; for I have heard them improvise stories by the night-fire sufficiently charged with horror as to make any piccaninny jump out of his skin – that is the wallaby one – and at other times their concoctions of the ludicrous have shaken the sides of listeners of both colours, and sent shouts of laughter into the otherwise silent forest They had a keen perception and vivid enjoyment of the ridiculous. I have heard Moullia, whom I have mentioned elsewhere, who after his return from Adelaide was esteemed by his countrymen much as we regard a distinguished explorer, give utterance to monstrous fabrications relating to the distant city, until his auditors were convulsed with laughter.

They evinced readiness and ingenuity in adopting expedients to meet sudden emergencies. On one occasion a small cutter, the *Governor Gawler*, had just sailed for Adelaide, when the captain's wife discovered that a small parcel containing documents of importance had been left behind. We made signals but the people on board did not recognise them as such. A fair wind had caught the sails, and I believed all chance of getting the parcel on board to be hopeless, when Mohudna, a tall athletic youth of about eighteen, offered to swim with it to the cutter. The wrapper consisted solely of brown paper, and there was not time to procure anything waterproof in addition to or instead of it; but Monkey, as we familiarly called him, undertook to deliver the package dry. Divesting himself of his apparel which with a savage is a very quick and simple process – he placed it on his head, and passing over it a thong of kangaroo tendon tied the latter securely under his chin and dashed into the water. Before he reached the cutter Monkey's head had become in appearance small and then undiscernible, so that we feared it and the documents had descended together to the fishes. At length we beheld him with assistance ascending the side of the ship, and after a momentary stay again descending to the water. On his head this time were half a dozen ship-biscuits, of which he became possessed through a degree of thoughtfulness which could not have been exceeded by a white messenger. He asked the recipient of the parcel how he should prove to those on shore that he had safely delivered it, and the captain gave him the readiest receipt at hand.

That the natives in all directions should be jealous of our encroachments is but natural, and the western tribes felt strongly on the subject. I was once sailing from Adelaide to Port Lincoln in very calm weather, and our small boat had to 'beat' along the western coast of Yorke's Peninsula. Occasionally we approached very close to the shore, and whenever we did so a large number of armed men and boys ran to the beach, and even some distance into the water, warning us by gestures and shouts not to land there. Some of the numerous spears which were thrown at us reached within a few yards of our deck. They made us distinctly understand two things, namely, to keep away from them, and to go on to Port Lincoln, where our countrymen were. Old Koongulta often argued with me very sensibly on the topic. He argued that having chosen Adelaide, with plenty of back country to 'sit down' on we might have kept away from Port Lincoln.

That they had attachments to scenes of their infancy I verified on several occasions. One instance will suffice. A very old man of the then scattered and nearly extinct Port Lincoln tribe was brought in a dying state and laid beneath the shadow of a particular tree close to my residence. The incident called for enquiry, and I found that he had with much solicitation induced his bearers, who were of another tribe, to take him to that spot, there to die and be buried, as it had been the scene of his boyhood. There they remained and tended him till his death. They then dug a very shallow grave, lowered him into it, and loosely filled it up with branches. I asked was there no funeral ceremony to ensue. Their answer was, 'He was not of our tribe,' and they at once took their departure. Their ordinary funeral ceremonies were sometimes very elaborate and long continued. I have known a body carried about on a sort of litter enveloped in foliage for several days, and then deposited permanently amid the branches of some patriarchal tree.

The mode adopted by the tribes in conferring names on new acquisitions by birth was precise and simple. A definite series of names existed both for males and females that came into use numerically, so that the first boy or third girl took at birth the appellation which custom prescribed for it. By this name the children were familiarly called. Another name was also acquired at birth which was derived from locality, being that of the river, tree, hill, or other designated object nearest to which the child was born. Those had the effect of our surnames and distinguished the fifth boy or the third girl of one family from the same numbered member of another. A third and final name was conferred on males when they approached sufficiently near to manhood to be admitted among warriors. The rites and ceremonies that accompanied that most important period in the lives of males were most elaborate, and prolonged for months. They involved the infliction of painful gashes and some mutilation, and were conducted with much solemnity and secrecy. Once a warrior, the native youth might distinguish himself by superior courage or ability, and thus win the respect and admiration of his fellows. But acts of skill, strength, daring, and agility would do no more. They would not confer command, for chieftainship was unknown among them.

To conclude this too lengthy article, the western tribes were favourable specimens of the race. I saw many men near Franklin Harbour and in other spots where fish and game were constantly abundant who exceeded six feet in height and were stout in proportion. In figure many of the youth, both male and female, might have served as models for a sculptor. I never observed in any of them traces of smallpox, which were not uncommon among the Adelaide and Encounter Bay tribes. They could not bear confinement. Subjected to it they pined and died. It was sometimes asserted that the natives were cannibals; but I never personally had proof of the fact, nor ever met with an individual who could supply conclusive evidence of it. That they sometimes killed their newborn infants is certain. A few instances of this dreadful act fell within my own knowledge. Except in one case the slaughtered infant was a twin. The mothers excused themselves by asserting that they could not do justice to two infants and the elder children also. The exceptional case was a half-caste whom the head of the family destroyed avowedly because of its complexion.

Had they a religion? I think not, if the word is to be considered in its true sense. The idea of becoming 'white-fellows' after death and other such absurdities were probably gleaned from Europeans. As far as I could gather, their belief or superstition was one of fear, not of hope; it consisted in dread of an evil spirit rather than in recognising the sovereignty of a good one. I well remember, one wild tempestuous day, when I had wandered a few miles from the settlement, seeing about seventy men, boys, women, and children running with the speed of deer.

They evinced extreme terror, shrieking, howling, and jabbering, with expanded eyes and streaming hair. Eventually they became invisible in a dense and tangled scrub. On their emerging, I ascertained that the evil spirit, whose name I forget, had just passed across the sky, and that therefore some great calamity would inevitably befall their tribe.

episode

XXII

South Australian Register 17 July 1878

THE FATAL JOURNEY OF C.C. DUTTON

When I travelled from Port Lincoln to Adelaide to report on the murder of Mr Brown and his hutkeeper in April of 1842, as previously mentioned, I was accompanied by Mr Charles Christian Dutton, who had decided to move his family, who had been residing for some time at the new settlement at Port Lincoln, back to the safety of Adelaide. Prior to their moving to Port Lincoln, I had known him intimately in Adelaide. He held the office of Sheriff prior to Mr Smart, who has been mentioned in connection with the criminal Magee.

A few weeks after I had returned once more to my new locality at Port Lincoln Mr Dutton arrived back there to take a herd of cattle belonging to the late Hon. John Baker back to Adelaide. To take cattle to Adelaide round the head of Spencer's Gulf, as he intended was an untried and eminently hazardous adventure, but Dutton was an old bushman and a dauntless man. The only previous attempt even to travel in that direction was made on foot by a man named Brown, who was never heard of again.

Mr Dutton left Port Lincoln in June, 1842. His companions were an old, New South Wales bushman named Cox; a young man named Graham, whose family were people of respectability at the west end of London; and two active and powerful middle-aged men, one a former Adelaide policeman named Brown, the other, I think, was called Haldane. It is a coincidence worth noting that among those individuals who lost their lives in attacks by natives at this disastrous period of the little settlement's history, three bore the last name of Brown, the first name in each case being John.

It was determined that an escort of friends should accompany the travellers through the country of the Battara tribe of blacks, members of which were unquestionably the perpetrators of the previous murders that had been committed. Accordingly Lieutenant Hugonin, two settlers in the district, and myself accompanied him for three days. The cattle were collected at Pillaworta - a small deserted station which had formerly been occupied by Mr Dutton, and which was situated some twenty or thirty miles from the starting point at Port Lincoln. His assistants had preceded him to Pillaworta and three or four soldiers were already stationed there. That was our resting-place the first night.

Having started at daybreak on good horses we lengthened our ride a few miles by going out of our direct route to visit the spots where Messrs. Brown and Biddle perished. We had solemn thoughts while engaged in contemplating the desolation caused by human violence amid a wilderness of life and beauty. The appearance of Mr Biddle's station more especially raised great feelings of sorrow, for he had made some progression in cultivation. He had grown wheat and established a garden containing English flowers, some of which still lived and flourished although human occupants had disappeared. The broken furniture and crockery, fragments of clothing, utensils, implements, &c., scattered around the dilapidated hut produced a degree of melancholy. There is something natural, however pathetic, in an old ruin where time has been the gradual innovator, but a promising work of human industry wantonly destroyed in its

EPISODE XXII

infancy is a mournful spectacle without mitigation. Dutton told me many minor incidents connected with the tragedy that until then had been unknown to me, and I could not help reflecting that he himself had just commenced a journey which would occupy many weeks through a wild and untracked country, known to be occupied by kinsmen of those whose diabolical work we were currently surveying. I had already entertained gloomy forebodings as to the issue of his undertaking, more especially as he and his party were poorly armed. The next day, the slow progress of the cattle and dray allowed ample time for erratic deviations from the route, to hunt small game which were available in great abundance and variety and presented frequent and irresistible temptations to stock the larder. That night we camped in a long, broken, irregular gully, in which were numerous small waterholes, some salt, others fresh. After one or two disappointments we were saved the trouble of testing the quality of the contents of any particular hole for we found that the best water was indicated by the remnants of aboriginal feasts such as parrots' feathers, and bones of kangaroo, wallaby, and fishes.

The night was very cold, but clear and starlit. Our cloaks and the frequently replenished fires kept us far from uncomfortable, and the evening passed pleasantly and cheerfully until we were all ready to bed down for the night. Just prior to preparing for bed, Mr Dutton went off to inspect the horses and cattle. We were just beginning to think his absence long when a tall, wild-looking figure, wrapped in a blanket and armed with what looked like a spear, appeared on the small rise at the edge of our camp-site. The somewhat startling apparition shouted a bloodcurdling native war cry. Instantly, Dutton's four men who were separately grouped, perhaps a hundred yards below us, sprang to their feet. From my own group a pistol appeared in the hands of Mr Hugonin and hunting rifles in other hands were cocked, levelled, and in another instant would almost certainly have been discharged, but vaguely recognising a familiar tone in that unearthly chant, I exclaimed 'Stop! 'Tis Dutton.' A loud laughing reply proved my statement to be correct. Poor Dutton, as tragic and melancholy as was his fate four or five days later, it would have been yet more mournful had he been felled by the hand of a friend, a victim of his own practical joke. The thought that obviously darted through every mind when the voice and figure of what was first thought to have been a crazed native assassin, was of course that Dutton, alone and unarmed, had been murdered.

Next morning my companions were again keen to do a little more hunting and sight-seeing before setting out on the return trip to Port Lincoln, while I, at Dutton's request, spent the morning in accompanying him as he moved the herd forward. We walked forward ahead of the stock and the baggage dray, leading our horses. I asked him as we started if he should not consult his compass. He replied that it was unnecessary, as the next forty miles to be traversed were familiar to him. He pointed to three conical hills in the distance which he said were his landmarks.

As this was the last we expected to see of each other for some considerable time we talked of many things – some discussions were of the future, some of events from the past, some jocular, but most of them serious. Noon was approaching when we were startled by sighting hoof-prints and wheel-ruts. They were extremely recent, and no wonder! They were the tracks made by ourselves that very morning! Dutton now consulted his compass, which confirmed the fact that in our progress we had wandered very far from a straight line. There were, we now noted, other conical hills that resembled his landmark sufficiently enough to mislead us when not attentively scrutinised.

EPISODE XXII

This had, without a doubt, been the cause of the mishap. Dutton now became somewhat dejected, and did not converse readily. The incident also impressed me as being a bad omen.

We soon after arrived at a water-hole, and Dutton ordered a halt, even though it was somewhat early for the midday meal. Although my companions were to have rejoined me by now to commence the homeward leg of our journey, we had not seen them since we parted from them, or rather they from us, very early in the morning. This was strange; but there was no telling to what extent our unfortunate digression had puzzled and misled them. We ate our meal thoughtfully, almost in silence. Clouds were gathering in dense dark masses, foreboding an early and very rainy evening. 'I shall not go any further today,' said Dutton, 'but make a long day's journey tomorrow. I am concerned about you, travelling home alone separated as you are from your party. You will find it difficult, in the heavy rain that is coming, to find your way either to Pillaworta or Port Lincoln, and in either case you have to pass through the lands of the Battaras.' He urged me earnestly to remain with him and not to start homeward, alleging that my companions would certainly find and follow the tracks of the herd, and rejoin us tomorrow at the very latest. Even in the unlikely event of my companions choosing to return to Port Lincoln rather than searching for the herd – the worst that could happen would be that I would have to suffer a few weeks with him and his crew in the bush and an unintended visit to Adelaide, but by attempting to journey back alone I was almost certain to be attacked by hostile blacks. The four men, who had now gathered round, seeing that I made preparation for departure, earnestly urged the same arguments. I however, adhered to my resolution, and about three o'clock was ready to start. Having shaken hands with all I mounted, experiencing meanwhile peculiarly painful feelings, for all were evidently in low spirits. 'Keep a good look out,' said Dutton as I left, 'and if you see any blacks give them a wide berth. On no account let them come near you. If you miss Pillaworta keep the Gulf in sight, and its coast will guide you to Port Lincoln. Good-bye; God bless you! I wish I could hear of your safe arrival home, but that I shall not be able to do until I reach Adelaide.' 'Don't be anxious about me,' I replied. 'I wish I was as confident of you reaching your destination safely as I am of arriving at mine.' And off I started at a sharp trot.

By this time the rain had begun to fall with that deliberate steadiness which implies that cessation is very far off, and in a few minutes it fell so closely that objects a few horse-lengths away from me were not discernible. I had proceeded about four miles when I heard a loud 'Cooee', which I felt certain issued from European lips, and to which I replied. After exchanging these calls for a few minutes to indicate our relative positions I joyfully rejoined my companions, who had lost all knowledge of their own, intended course while searching for me. Fortunately, the horse on which I rode had spent much of its lifetime at Pillaworta, and obviously had considerable liking for the sweet feed and clear water which were abundant there. From the free and unhesitating way in which he chose his course, I was certain that he contemplated heading directly to the comforts of a warm stable and abundant feed at that spot, which was many miles nearer to us than Port Lincoln. Accordingly 'Bobby' - he was the Resident's favourite horse - was unanimously elected pilot and I rode first of a single file. We were obliged to adopt this order of progress, for many of the strange places, no doubt short cuts, which the horse led us through would not admit two abreast. The rain fell heavily and ceaselessly. Water rushed over the horses' hoofs and descended in cascades from the trees. Much of our way was thickly wooded, and at times I could see little beyond Bobby's ears. The manner in which he conducted the expedition produced some discomfort to the riders. He evidently considered directness of route and speed as of more importance than level ground and free passage for his rider's head, and consequently our faces were occasionally mopped by very wet branches.

Having ridden on for what appeared an unreasonable time without recognising anything indicative of our destination, my companions began to seriously question Bobby's skill in the art of navigation, so we paused a minute or two to consult on our predicament. My confidence in the horse was unshaken, because there was none of that twirling of ears, sidelong looks at his rider, and other symptoms of dubiousness which a horse displays when he is ignorant of the road himself, and begins to suspect that the rider is in the same dilemma. I again urged Bobby forward and left the rein on his neck, when away he went on the same track as before, and after a gradual ascent of about a mile we glimpsed a mass of red light about two miles ahead. We took care to ensure that it was not a natives' fire, and then the space being open, on we dashed. The soldiers, stationed at Pillaworta having become alarmed at our long absence, had kindled an enormous pile of wood outside the hut as a signal fire, and anticipating the cold and wet condition in which we should arrive, had been equally unsparing in their efforts to maintain the huge fire within the hut. What great luxury it seemed, to have a roof over our heads, a sea-pie supper and a dry blanket on a warm floor that night. Lying warm and comfortable within the shelter of the cabin my thoughts, before sleep overtook me, were for those we had left in the inhospitable bush and of the weary miles of wilderness that lay before them. Poor fellows! About five days after that they were all dead men, while I, about whom they expressed so much anxiety, arrived safely at Port Lincoln next day.

While the details of the events were fresh in my memory I composed the following sonnet, which I dedicated to those men.

The Desert Meal

Four hundred miles through the bush crowded waste
Christian essayed a lowing herd to guide,
With four adventurous helpers at his side.
Friends cheered his outset, who too keenly chased
The wind-swift game till them no more we traced,
And I alone did with the bushmen ride.
We paused by a ravine, gloomy and wide,
Choked with dwarfed trees and shrubs close interlaced.
There ate we, for pure water gushed hard by.
'Farewell!' said Christian, 'fifty miles are spread
'Twixt you and home — miles where in ambush lie
Wild men with hands from recent murders red!'
We parted — I to live, those five to die.
That desert ne'er restored them, quick or dead!

Week after week passed away and month after month, yet nothing was heard of the five travellers. The limited communication then maintained between settlers and the natives furnished equally little information regarding Dutton's overland party but the few small rumours that did manage to filter through were most unfavourable. The visits of the small cutter which was then the only reliable medium of communication between the Port Lincoln settlement and Adelaide were generally from two to three months apart, and I have known even more than sixteen weeks elapse without a word of intelligence being received from any quarter; either by letter or newspaper. Thus we were not aware of the non-arrival of Dutton and his party until three months after they should have arrived in

EPISODE XXII

Adelaide. Then orders arrived from Adelaide for the formation of a party at Port Lincoln to proceed in search of them. Having not already received word of Dutton's arrival in Adelaide, the Government Resident had by that time decided to organise a search party from the Port on his own initiative.

episode

XXIII

South Australian Register 31 July 1878

UNSUCCESSFUL SEARCH FOR DUTTON

A party was immediately formed to search the coast of Spencer's Gulf for Mr Dutton and his missing companions. The plan adopted was to charter a whaleboat, sail up the Gulf, anchor each night, and penetrate inland every ensuing morning until the track of the cattle party should be arrived at. It was known that Dutton meant to keep as near the coast as practicable. Accordingly a whaleboat was engaged, the owner undertaking to accompany and manage it. As many barrels and kegs of water as the boat could contain while still maintaining sufficient space for other absolutely indispensable articles were stowed in her.

The party consisted of five persons – the owner of the boat, the local Protector of Aborigines, two gentlemen from Adelaide – Mr Charles George Hawker and Mr James Baker – and myself, who represented the Government Resident, he being indisposed at the time. Owing to the necessity for laying in a good supply of water and eatables, when the weight of the passengers was added the boat sank extremely low in the water. It was therefore necessary for the living cargo to distribute itself so as to best to accommodate the dead weight, of the supplies. The result was a variety of human positions that looked far more grotesque than graceful. We fortunately had time enough on shore daily to uncramp our limbs.

The weather during our voyage, which lasted more than three weeks, was generally squally and tempestuous, with heavy storms of rain. The latter was not an unmixed evil; for although it drenched our garments by day, it also enabled us to economise on our stock of water, and occasionally to collect enough from the granite basins of the rocks to replenish a keg or two.

Landing on, and getting off the coast were operations of considerable difficulty and involved some danger. In rough weather there is a heavy surf on the western shore of Spencer's Gulf. It was considered necessary to place the boat high and dry every night, because, separated from it, our position would have been critical. As it was also necessary to lighten the boat before running her ashore, we often had to wade a considerable distance and this was a tedious and disagreeable process. Often the water rose to the waist, sometimes to the chin, and occasionally it was not easy to maintain a footing. Being of somewhat shorter stature, I was often indebted to Mr Hawker for aid in scrambling to and from the boat.

The first day a fair wind carried us as far as Tumby Island, about twenty-five miles distant from Port Lincoln, and there we remained all night. The next, we made about fifteen miles, also a good day's progress considering the laden condition of our little vessel. On the third day we encountered a contrary wind and could not resume our voyage – a circumstance which we did not totally regret as it gave us time to reflect on the beauty of our surroundings. The day was hot, but we had the sea-breeze and an abundance of natural shade cast by growing and prostrate trees. Some of the latter formed the framework of arbours, which a variety of neighbouring trailing plants walled and roofed delightfully, working into the texture of wild honeysuckle and other indigenous flowers. A grassy carpet and fallen stems of trees served for excellent lounges, and we luxuriated on them for a few hours to our hearts' content. In the forenoon, accompanied by one of the party, I walked about a mile and a half inland, and again in the afternoon we walked perhaps a couple of miles along the margin of the Gulf. We were returning to our leafy camp when we observed about a quarter of a mile inland several natives painted and armed. They were about an equal distance from us and from our small encampment, forming as it were the third point of a triangle. They advanced gradually towards the Gulf in a bending position, evidently examining the ground with attention. We knew at once that our footprints of the morning were guiding them surely although slowly to our comrades. Descending from the edge of the cliff to the beach, we ran rather than walked to our encampment, where we found our comrades comfortably dozing, unapprehensive of danger. Through the narrow gaps of our fragrant shelter we beheld the natives stealthily approaching. A very few minutes sufficed to secure our moveables in the boat and float her off in charge of her owner. Then all four of us, fully armed, issued from our ambush towards our unwelcome visitors, who, the moment they saw us, uttered a short sharp exclamation, wheeled round, and disappeared like a flight of arrows. We kept a good watch throughout the remainder of the day, but saw no more of them.

One gusty rainy afternoon, about the usual time for landing, we were off a peculiarly rough bit of coast About two miles ahead was a point running some distance into the Gulf, beyond which we thought there might be a sheltered smooth little bay better adapted for our landing, in which case we would have prolonged our voyage, even at the risk of landing in the dusk. Mr Hawker volunteered to swim ashore, cross the tongue of land, and ascertain if such a desirable haven existed there. He had stripped, and was just about to plunge over the bow, when I called 'Stop! A shark.' An enormous fish of that species passed close beneath our keel, and six others presented themselves the instant afterwards.

We determined to land at once rather than make a prolonged effort with no certainty of a favourable result. We were wet with surf and rain and numbed with cold. Landing the boat and her cargo that evening was unusually harassing. To make matters even worse, it was my job to light a fire. Every article from the boat, including matches, was sodden with salt water or fresh or both, and as everything ashore, including gum leaves, was dripping with rain, my task was no easy one. It occupied me an hour. The miseries of the process I committed to writing shortly afterwards, but am not going to insert them here.

We spent one day, when the wind was adverse, in Franklin Harbour. The surface of the water was smooth, and its body as clear as crystal. The finny world beneath carried on its multiform operations under our inspection. The scene was a most extraordinary one. Fishes in prodigious numbers, of all sizes, and fifty different species, were gliding and darting about, yet so massed together were they that some skill appeared to be necessary to avoid collision with each other. We made fishing our occupation, but sport it was not. The results were far too substantial for that. Snapper was our quarry, of which a large shoal was in the bay, and as fast as the lines descended the bait was taken. In two instances sharks did us the honour to respond to invitations not intended for them, and of course took away with them tackle as well as bait. A third line and hook we lost just as a fine snapper was secured through a shark swallowing him at the very instant of his capture.

Hitherto every journey inland had resulted in our reaching Mr Dutton's track, and on the seventeenth day after sailing we reached the neighbourhood of Middleback Mountain about one hundred and thirty miles from Port Lincoln. We saw the reflection of numerous fires of natives, and on ascending a tree near the coast counted upwards of sixty. For the last few days numerous signal fires had arisen from time to time in advance of us, and from these and other indications we concluded that we were not far from the point ultimately reached by Dutton. That night, for safety, the boat was kept afloat, her owner remaining in her. The blacks reconnoitred both him and us, as was evident from the number of flitting fire-sticks which the darkness made plainly perceptible in all directions. We took the precaution of watching in turns. On the following morning at daybreak we deposited all our chattels in the boat, and directed that she should be kept well off land until our return. It was well we did so, for several attempts were made on the boat in our absence. Spears were thrown from the shore, and parties of swimmers now and again attempted to capture her. At one time she was surrounded by swimmers, but the pointing of a double-barrel gun at the leaders obtained time for the boatman to pull beyond their reach.

Our party, after seeing the boat fairly afloat, struck in a direct line inland. The day was remarkably bright, uncomfortably so for the rays of the sun exhaling the previous day's rain in the midst of a tall thick scrub rendered the atmosphere oppressively close. Flies settled on us in clouds and tormented us much. We were heavily armed, bathed in perspiration, and had neither hand at liberty to contend with swarms of buzzing and tickling insects. As nearly as we could estimate we penetrated fifteen miles inland. On our way we encountered no natives, but at frequent intervals beheld signs of their hurried retreat, such as skins and food left around freely burning fires. Noon arrived, yet we had neither tasted nor seen water since we drained the flasks we had carried with us, although we must have unknowingly passed many waterholes, for without an abundance of water, such numbers of natives could not have congregated. At last we saw a small spring glistening in a hollow surrounded by higher ground, which in shape resembled a funnel. Most incautiously all four descended. We found a tiny

EPISODE XXIII

reservoir, so shallow that our pannikins were almost useless. I had scooped out and swallowed the contents of a percussion cap-box thrice replenished, when the thought of our incaution struck me. 'We have entered a natural trap,' I said; 'take your turn, and I will go up again now.' I had occasion to signal my companions to come up immediately, for crouching savages were stealing on us like cats on all sides. They, however, immediately disappeared. We now diverged a little from our line of return, thinking we might shorten our distance from the boat, and on entering a small green open space, surrounded by gumtrees, we came, evidently by surprise, on about thirty natives, who, the moment we appeared, scattered themselves like mist, and were lost in the surrounding scrub. Their dinners – some still in the process of being cooked, and others partly demolished – were left behind. So were a large number of spears and waddies. One very old man was so frightened that instead of making off towards some definite point of the compass he ran or rather hobbled to and fro. We considered this a fortunate incident, in as much as it would probably enable us to obtain information respecting the objects of our search. We therefore took the old man with us. Mr Baker suggested that we should place the numerous wooden weapons which lay around us on the fires, which were burning briskly. I advised the contrary, arguing that the destruction of them could not benefit us while hundreds of others were in the hands of natives around us, and that such an act of aggression might provoke a confrontation endangering ourselves and tending to defeat the object of our journey. From our prisoner, perhaps, we might obtain the intelligence we sought.

As we proceeded cries and shouts of natives arose on every side, the screams of women predominating. On arriving at an open space we paused, and made signs that we were not to be followed. A tall, athletic young warrior laid down his weapons and motioned that he wished to approach us alone. We assented. On his reaching us he made us understand that he wished us to release the old man and receive him as captive instead. This was a strange proposal. My own impression was that the old man was of unsound mind and regarded with superstitious reverence by his tribe; at all events, on the exchange being agreed to he departed, exhibiting many symptoms of idiocy, and was received by his younger tribesmen with great demonstrations of joy. During our journey to the coast we suffered greatly from fatigue and intensely from thirst. On arrival we saw our boat was a long way off, and no water was obtainable until it reached the shore. After a much needed supper of tea and damper we fed our prisoner, lashed him to a log near the fire, supplied him with a capacious blanket, and arranged to take in turn an hour's watch. The boat was hauled close to us, and its owner undertook not to move from it.

I had to keep watch from eleven to twelve. On being aroused from a most determined slumber by my sentinel predecessor, I walked quickly a few paces to and fro, drank a pannikin of tea, and adopted other means to resist the drowsiness that beset me. On the opposite side of the fire from that where I sat lay the prisoner apparently asleep, but I believed him to be watchfully awake and therefore checked drowsiness to the utmost. I began to wish for the arrival of midnight, looked at my watch, and found that only twelve minutes had to elapse. The black was still in the same slumberous attitude. I became conscious of a momentary droop of the head, started up, and found that the prisoner was gone. I rushed from the fire with my rifle, hoping to catch sight of the fugitive, but in vain. I then aroused the boat-keeper, and next my successor in the watch. I was greatly annoyed at this event. Our remaining load of provisions had been confined to a blanket and a towel, which latter article must have been snatched off a shrub by the rascal as he passed; but the greatest loss was the chance of ascertaining from him the fate of Dutton.

As we had not crossed his track during this last journey it was obvious that the dray at least might be found between that point and the one last occupied by us. We longed to solve the problem, but to do so was impracticable. Our stock of meat had long since been exhausted, and as far as food was concerned we had subsisted for some days entirely on seabirds, periwinkles, and mutton-fish. Although we had to some extent used indigenous roots in an effort to economise on flour, our supplies of which had now been entirely consumed and our water kegs were nearly empty. So we had no option but to steer for home, bearing the inconclusive intelligence that the party with their dray had passed one defined spot and had not reached another some miles beyond. We regained Port Lincoln on the twenty-second day after our departure.

Before we left Port Lincoln, Dutton's horse and several head of cattle had found their way back to Pillaworta. Shortly after that, a native of a neighbouring tribe came forward with information regarding the fate of the party. I had no doubt at all as to the accuracy of his story. Having accompanied Dutton's party for three days I had sufficient knowledge of their mode of proceeding to test the genuineness of his narrative. He described the five individuals with surprising exactness. Of Dutton's height he gave me a very good idea with his hand, and brought to my mind some minute peculiarities of his countenance. Cox's relative shortness he correctly described, and that individual being very much pitted with smallpox, he vividly described that deformity by touching his face in several places with the tip of a forefinger. With similar readiness he described the others. Of course I conducted the man to the settlement, and his statement was recorded in the Courthouse.

The narrative amounted to this. One day, towards sundown,

Dutton and Cox were in advance of the other members of the party. It was their custom while I travelled with them for one or both to precede the dray and cattle immediately after the midday meal, in search of a suitable camping place for the night. On this occasion they must have been later than usual in halting, probably because they could not readily find water. Dutton and Cox came across a party of native women, who were making preparations to encamp for the night, from which circumstances might be inferred the fact that water was not far distant. The women, on seeing the white faces, started off like so many startled deer, except one whom Dutton detained by the wrists. The whole of them commenced a shrill piercing shriek that is common on such occasions, and which I have heard in the stillness of evening at a distance of four miles.

It resembles the steam whistle of a railway locomotive more than any other sound I am acquainted with. The men of the tribe suddenly appeared on all sides, abandoning their game, spears, and skin garments, they rushed to the rescue of the woman and killed the two white men with their waddies. Haldane then came up with the dray and shared a similar fate. The tragedy was completed on arrival of Graham and Brown with the cattle, the fatal waddies inflicting a painful and bloody death to them also.

NOTES

[1] South-eastern corner of King William Street and North Terrace intersection
[2] South-western corner of King William Street and North Terrace intersection
[3] The O G was a 28 foot cutter of 9 tons, altered in 1848 to 35 foot and 12 tons. It was wrecked at Poole's Flat near Second Valley in 1854.
[4] The author, Nathaniel Hailes, and the satirist, Timothy Short, were in fact the same person.
[5] Newspapers of the day indicate that Nultia was executed on 7 April, 1843 in front of the ruins of Mr Biddle's house, about twenty miles from Port Lincoln while Narrabie was publicly hanged in front of the entrance to the Adelaide Gaol on 1 August, 1843. Both names were spelt in a variety of ways.

AUTHOR'S NOTE

During the process of compiling this collection of Nathaniel Hailes's works I had the honour to meet, and to be assisted by Ms Bronwen Jones who kindly let me see photographs and information pertaining to her great-grandfather, Nathaniel Hailes, and his family.

I was also privileged to meet well-known author and historian Mr Keith Borrow, who provided me with information that was available to him, and went out of his way to locate additional sources of relevant material. I am also indebted to Mr Borrow for the voluntary use of his photographic skills.

Ms Juliana Bayfield of the State Library of South Australia provided much factual information that was of great benefit to my research.

I am deeply indebted also to Mr Peter Price of the History Teachers Association of South Australia for his valued comments and encouragement.

My wife Pauline and daughters Ani and Leeza each spent many hours in helping to type this work and greatly encouraged me with their enthusiasm.

To all these people and to all those friends and neighbours who assisted with proofreading, my heartfelt appreciation is warmly extended.

Allan L. Peters, Adelaide, 1998

INDEX

Adelphi 4
Advocate-General 11, 99, 103
America 1, 28
Andrews 131
Angas, George Fife 24
      George French 152
Anglified natives 31
Anglo-Saxon 29
Ashton, Mr 53
Australia 1, 26, 57, 63, 71-2, 74, 81, 129
Baker, Hon. John 159
    M. James 168, 173
Bank of South Australia 15, 84
Battara (Gumscrub) Tribe 117, 160, 163
Bay Road 96
Beevor, Captain 146
Biddle, Charles 111-4, 117, 135, 146, 160, 177
Birmingham 4, 5
Black Forrest 50
Black Thursday 81
Blenkinsop, Captain 13
Bobby 164-5
Bond Street 106
Bonny, Mr 45
Boston Bay 107-9, 117, 124, 130, 132, 136-8, 140
  Island 138-9, 141, 151
Bow Street 53
Brien, Bill 128-31, 133-4
Brown Bess 55
Brown, John 20, 109-10, 112, 117, 135, 159-60, 176
  Street 11
Buckinghamshire 3-5
Buffalo Row 10
Burnside 38, 40

Burra 61
Byron, Lord 72, 76
Calcutta 107
Campbell, Colonel 1
Cape Jaffa 42
Central Africa 61
Chambers, Mr 67
Chambers' Stables 67
Chief Justice 48, 52-3
Clerk of the Court 106-7
    to Government Resident 106
Colonial Secretary 16
Cooper, Chief Justice 13, 48, 53-4
Coorong 43-4
Coroner 48, 66
Corroboree 30-1
Councillor 102
Cox 159, 175-6
Crusoe, Robinson 10, 38, 123
Curran, John Philpot 6
Dandie Dinmont 6
Darke, Mr 143-6
Davis, A.H. 1
Denham, Mr 46
  Mrs 46
Deptford 4
Driver, Charles John 107
Dry Creek 11
Duff, Captain 17-8
Dutton, Charles Christian 143, 159-64, 166-68, 171-2, 175-6
East Indies 107
East Terrace 20
Egypt 148
Elles, Mr 6-7
Emerald Isle 108, 129

Encounter Bay Tribe 157
Encounter Bay 37, 41-3, 65-8, 143, 157
England 1-3, 16-7, 43, 53-4, 71, 74, 78, 82, 85-6, 103, 112, 114
Europe 24, 55, 61, 63, 71, 77, 130
Eyre, Mr 18
Fanny 41-2
Fastins 112-4
Finlay, Dr 18
Fisher, Sir James Hurtle 98, 99
Flinders Island 129-31
Flinders, Matthew 21, 106, 129, 137, 141
Forster, Mr Anthony 56
Franklin Harbour 157, 171
Franklin 141
    Lady 21, 141-2
Gawler, Colonel 20-21, 37, 44-5, 95, 97-9, 104-5
Gawler River 37
Gawler (Town) 18, 34-5
Germany 26
Gilbert Street 12, 16, 20
Giles, William 1
Gill, Captain 42
Gilles Arcade 14, 16, 19
Gilles, Osmond 10, 14, 17, 38, 95, 99
Glen Osmond 38
Glenelg 6, 8, 29, 95, 107
Gofton, John 48, 50-6
Goolwa 43, 61
Gosse, Dr 15
Gouger, Robert 1-3, 16
    Mrs 16
Government House 19-20, 22, 45
  Resident 21, 106-9, 140, 164, 167-8
  Store 19
Governor Gawler 154
Governor 6, 13, 19-21, 28, 34, 44-5, 52, 97, 99, 103, 105, 137
Graham 159, 176
Gravesend 5

Great Britain 123
Grenfell Street 12
Grey, Captain 105, 106, 137
Hack, Mr 10
Hahndorf 27
Hailes, Nathaniel 6, 177
Haldane 160, 176
Happy Valley 137-8
Hart, Captain 18, 68
Harvey, Dr 121, 138-40
    Mrs 139-40
Hawker, Charles George 168-70
Hawson, Francis 109, 152
Hill, Rowland 4, 78
Hindley Street 97-8
Hindmarsh Island 13
Hindmarsh, Captain 20, 97
Hobart Town 43
Holdfast Bay 5-6, 29, 108, 137
Horseshoe, (Noarlunga) 61
House of Lords 3
Hugonin, Lieutenant 135-6, 160-1
Hume, Joseph 78
Hutchinson 13
Ireland 131, 133
Island of St Pauls 5
Islington 51
James, Horton 2, 9, 30
Jeffcott, Sir John 13
Jickling, Mr 13-4
Joe Manton 55
Kangaroo Island 5-6
Kapunda 61
Kavel, Mr 26
Kensington 30, 38, 40, 43, 62
King George Sound 42
King William Street 15, 19, 77, 98, 177
Kirton Point 128-9
Klemzig 24-5, 27, 30
Koongulta 151, 155
Lake Victoria 67, 69

Lamb, Charles 73-4
Light, Colonel 11, 20
Little Para 35
Lobethal 27
Lomas, Trooper J.B. 51, 53-5
London, 3-5, 77, 104, 159
Longbottom, Mrs 42
           Rev. Mr 42
Lovelock, Joseph 110-11
MacDonnell, Mr 109
Maderia 5
Magee, Michael 48-9, 65, 159
Mann, Charles 11-2, 52, 84, 99, 103
Maria 41-3, 45-6, 146
Marino 62
McFarlane, Mr 18
McPherson, Mr 21
Middle Island 131
Middleback Mountain 171
Milliltie 152
Milmenrura 146
Mohudna 154-5
Montefiore Hill 11
Morgan, (William) 48-9, 65-6
Morphett Street 11, 51
Moullia 154
Mount Barker 38, 62, 83
Mount Lofty 11, 50, 83, 85, 99
Municipal Council 98, 99, 101-2
Murray River 13, 41
Murray Street 36
Murray Tribes 31
Narrabie 114, 177
Nash, Dr 12
New South Wales 29, 73, 81, 123, 144, 159
New Zealand 1, 29
Nicholls, Mr 66-8
North Adelaide 15, 24, 34, 51
North Africa 85
North American Indians 29
North Park Lands 49

North Pole 61
North Terrace 15, 19, 61, 84, 177
Norwood 62, 85
Nultia 114, 177
O'Halloran, Major 44-5, 67, 69
           Mrs 70
O'Halloran's Well 69-70
Obootoo 148
OG 95, 177
Old Spot, (Hotel) 34, 36
Para River 36, 48, 50-2
Parcell, William 16
Park Lands 10, 19, 23, 29
Pillaworta 160, 163-5, 175
Police Commissioner 44, 45, 67
Poole's Flat 177
Port Adelaide 43, 62-3
Port Darwin 63
Port Lincoln 21, 29, 45, 106, 109-10, 112, 117,
      126-7, 141, 143-6, 148, 150, 152, 155,
      159-60, 162-7, 169, 171, 175, 177
Porter, Captain 136
Portland Place 10
Portsmouth 5
Post Office 19, 24, 71, 77-8
Pratt 37
Prince Albert 99
Protector of Aboriginals 150, 168
Prussia 23
Pullen, Mr 43, 45
Reedbeds 1
Register 54
Resident Magistrate 107
Rivoli Bay 43
Rodney 6
Rufus 29
Rugby 5
Rush 138
Scotland 69
Shakespeare 59, 76
Sheriff 48-9, 97, 159

Short, Timothy 99, 177
Smart, Samuel 48-9, 159
Smith, Captain 46
South Adelaide 11, 51
South Australia 2-3, 13, 19, 21, 29, 43, 56, 61, 72, 74, 79-81, 103, 123, 130, 137
South Australian Company 1, 10, 19, 39, 95, 109
South Australian Gazette and *Colonial Register* 41
South-Eastern Tribes 44
Southern Districts 67
Spencer's Gulf 107, 117, 123, 124, 135, 141, 159, 168-70
St Johns Church 14
St Vincent's Gulf 35
Stagg, Joseph 48, 50-5
Stamford Hill 141
Stanley, Lord 2
Stephens Place 15
Stock Keeper Inn 36
Strangways 13
Sturt, Captain 1, 10-11
Supreme Court 19
Sussex 6
Tasmania 17, 29, 42-43, 53, 141, 144
Theakstone, Mr 143-6
Thebarton 20

Thomas, Mr 10
Tolmer, Inspector 45, 50
Torrens River 2, 9, 15, 24-25, 29, 64, 102
Torrens, Colonel 4
Treasurer 99
Treasury 19
Tubbs, Charles 112-4
    Mrs 113-4
Tumby Island 169
United Kingdom 78
Unley 30
Utulta 153
Van Diemem's Land 17, 50, 66, 123
Victoria 29, 74, 81
Walkerville 30
Waterloo 97, 104
Watson, Mr 18
Watts, Captain 77
Wellington, Duke of 2-3, 97
West Terrace 16
Western Australia 42, 54, 105
Western Tribe 149
Wigley, Mr 107
Wilkins, Peter 59
Willunga 61, 66-7
York, James 43, 46
    Mrs 46
Yorke's Peninsula 155

Wakefield Press is an independent publishing and
distribution company based in Adelaide, South Australia.
We love good stories and publish beautiful books.
To see our full range of books, please visit our website at
www.wakefieldpress.com.au
where all titles are available for purchase.
To keep up with our latest releases, news and events,
subscribe to our monthly newsletter.

Find us!

Facebook: www.facebook.com/wakefield.press
Twitter: www.twitter.com/wakefieldpress
Instagram: www.instagram.com/wakefieldpress

www.ingramcontent.com/pod-product-compliance
Lightning Source LLC
Chambersburg PA
CBHW032135160426
43197CB00008B/656